Disability in the UK

Editor: Tina Brand

Volume 327

Independence Educational Publishers

First published by Independence Educational Publishers

The Studio, High Green

Great Shelford

Cambridge CB22 5EG

England

ISBN-13: 978 1 86168 778 4

Printed in Great Britain

Zenith Print Group

Contents

Introduction

DISABILITY IN THE UK is Volume 327 in the **ISSUES** series. The aim of the series is to offer current, diverse information about important issues in our world, from a UK perspective.

ABOUT DISABILITY IN THE UK

The term disability covers a wide range of physical, psycho-social, sensory or intellectual impairments which may or may not affect a person's ability to carry out their day-to-day activities. This book explores the issues disabled people face in their everyday lives. It takes a look at the lives of young carers. It also considers the issue of accessibility to areas such as sports stadiums, shops, buses and trains. In addition to this it explores disability in the workplace.

OUR SOURCES

Titles in the **ISSUES** series are designed to function as educational resource books, providing a balanced overview of a specific subject.

The information in our books is comprised of facts, articles and opinions from many different sources, including:

⇨ Newspaper reports and opinion pieces

⇨ Website factsheets

⇨ Magazine and journal articles

⇨ Statistics and surveys

⇨ Government reports

⇨ Literature from special interest groups.

A NOTE ON CRITICAL EVALUATION

Because the information reprinted here is from a number of different sources, readers should bear in mind the origin of the text and whether the source is likely to have a particular bias when presenting information (or when conducting their research). It is hoped that, as you read about the many aspects of the issues explored in this book, you will critically evaluate the information presented.

It is important that you decide whether you are being presented with facts or opinions. Does the writer give a biased or unbiased report? If an opinion is being expressed, do you agree with the writer? Is there potential bias to the 'facts' or statistics behind an article?

ASSIGNMENTS

In the back of this book, you will find a selection of assignments designed to help you engage with the articles you have been reading and to explore your own opinions. Some tasks will take longer than others and there is a mixture of design, writing and research-based activities that you can complete alone or in a group.

Useful weblinks

www.arthritiscare.org.uk

www.bma.org.uk

www.carers.org

www.centreforsocialjustice.org.uk

www.dyspraxiafoundation.org.uk

www.fabians.org.uk

www.huffingtonpost.com

www.ilo.org

www.independent.co.uk

www.innovation.ox.ac.uk

www.lse.ac.uk

www.nhs.uk

www.nursingtimes.net

www.papworthtrust.org.uk

www.publications.parliament.uk

www.research-information, bristol.ac.uk

www.telegraph.co.uk

www.theconversation.com

www.theguardian.com

FURTHER RESEARCH

At the end of each article we have listed its source and a website that you can visit if you would like to conduct your own research. Please remember to critically evaluate any sources that you consult and consider whether the information you are viewing is accurate and unbiased.

Disability: Facts

The term disability covers a wide range of different physical, psycho-social, sensory or intellectual impairments which may or may not affect a person's ability to carry out their day-to-day activities, including their jobs.

Women and men with disabilities work in all sectors of the economy and in all types of roles. Many have demonstrated that with the right opportunities and adjustment, where required, to a job or the work environment, they can make a valuable contribution to the world of work.

Facts about people with disabilities

⇨ One billion of the world's population, or 15 per cent, live with a disability (WHO, WB 2011).

⇨ Disabled people are at a higher risk of poverty in every country, whether measured in traditional economic indicators relative to GDP or, more broadly, in non-monetary aspects of living

standards such as education, health and living conditions.

⇨ Disabled women are at greater risk of poverty than men with disabilities (Mitra et al. 2011). Their poverty is linked to their very limited opportunities for education and skills development. Approximately 785 million women and men with disabilities are of working age, but the majority do not work. When they do work, they earn less than people without disabilities but further gender disparities exist. Women with disabilities earn less than men with disabilities.

⇨ According to an ILO pilot study of ten low- and middle-income developing countries, excluding people with disabilities from the labour force results in estimated GDP losses ranging from three and seven per cent (Buckup 2009).

⇨ People with disabilities are frequently excluded from education, vocational training and employment opportunities.

⇨ 51 per cent of young boys with disabilities completed primary school, compared with 61 per cent of young boys without disabilities, based on World Health Organization (WHO) surveys in more than fifty countries. In the same survey, girls with disabilities reported 42 per cent primary

school completion compared with 53 per cent of girls without disabilities (WHO, WB 2011).

⇨ Disability affects not only the person with a disability, but also their families. Many family members who provide primary care to another family member with a disability have often left work due to their caring responsibilities. What is more, carers and the families of people with disabilities usually experience a higher level of financial hardship than the general population (Inclusion International 2007).

References

World Health Organization and the World Bank: World Report on Disability, 2011.

- Mitra et al. 2011. Disability and Poverty in Developing Countries: A snapshot from the World Health Survey. *SP Discussion Paper*, World Bank.

- Buckup, S. 2009. The price of exclusion: The economic consequences of excluding people with disabilities from the world of work, *Employment Working Paper No. 43*, International Labour Organization, Geneva.

- Inclusion International. 2007. "The Human Rights of Adults with Learning Disabilities", Report submitted to The Joint Committee on Human Rights Committee Office, House of Commons, 24 May 2007, p. 2.

November 2016

⇨ The above information is reprinted with kind permission from the International Labour Organization. Please visit www.ilo.org for further information.

© 2018 International Labour Organization

Disability in the United Kingdom 2016 facts and figures

An extract from an article by the Papworth Trust.

Key statistics

⇨ There are around 11.9 million disabled people in the UK. Almost one in five people (19%) in the UK have a disability; this figure has remained relatively constant over time (12.2 million in 2012/13).[1]

⇨ The prevalence of disability rises with age: in 2012/13, 7% of children were disabled (0.9 million), compared to 16% of adults of working age (6.1 million), and 42% of adults over state pension age (5.1 million). There are more disabled women than men in the UK.[2]

⇨ In 2014/15, the most common impairments that disabled people had were: mobility (57%), stamina/breathing/fatigue (38%), dexterity (28%) and mental health (16%). Some people had more than one impairment but were asked to identify which one had the most impact on daily life.[3]

⇨ The distribution of disabled people is fairly evenly spread across the UK. The North East, Wales, the North West and East Midlands have the highest rates of disability, while London, the South East and the East of England have the lowest.[4]

⇨ People from white ethnic groups are almost twice as likely as those from non-white ethnic groups to have a limiting long-standing illness or disability (20% compared with 11%).[5]

⇨ Disabled people are less likely to be in employment. In January 2016, the UK employment rate among working age disabled people was 46.5% (4.1 million), compared to 84%% of non-disabled people.[6]

⇨ 44.3% of working age disabled people are economically inactive. This figure is nearly four times higher than for nondisabled people (11.5 %).[7]

⇨ The two most commonly stated needs for employment among adults with impairments are modified hours or days or reduced work hours, and tax credits.[8]

⇨ The two most common barriers to work amongst adults with impairments are a lack of job opportunities (43%) and difficulty with transport (29%).[9]

⇨ Disabled adults are nearly three times as likely as non-disabled adults to have no formal qualifications, 30% and 11% respectively.[10]

⇨ The two main barriers to educational opportunities for disabled adults are finance (15%) and a health condition, illness or impairment (9%).[11]

⇨ 19% of households that include a disabled person live in relative income poverty (below 60% of median income), compared to 14% of households without a disabled person.[12]

⇨ The gap of people in absolute low income between families where at least one member is disabled and those where no-one is disabled has increased over the last few years.[13]

⇨ The largest gap is amongst working-age adults in families with at least one disabled person (22% compared to 12%).[14]

⇨ The high level of unemployment is the primary reason why so man

1. Department for Work and Pensions, July 2014, Family Resources Survey 2012/13, (online), available at: https://www.gov.uk/government/uploads/system/uploads/attachment_data/file/325491/familyresources-survey-statistics-2012-2013.pdf

2. Department for Work and Pensions, July 2014, Family Resources Survey 2012/13, (online), available at: https://www.gov.uk/government/uploads/system/uploads/attachment_data/file/325491/familyresources-survey-statistics-2012-2013.pdf

3. Department for Work and Pensions, July 2014, Family Resources Survey 2012/13, (online), available at: https://www.gov.uk/government/uploads/system/uploads/attachment_data/file/325491/familyresources-survey-statistics-2012-2013.pdf

4. Department for Work and Pensions, July 2014, Family Resources Survey 2012/13, (online), available at: https://www.gov.uk/government/uploads/system/uploads/attachment_data/file/325491/familyresources-survey-statistics-2012-2013.pdf

5. Office for National Statistics, 2014, Adult Health in Great Britain, 2012, (online), available at: http://www.ons.gov.uk/ons/dcp171778_355938.pdf http://www.ons.gov.uk/ons/datasetsand-tables/index.html?pageSize=50&sortBy=none&sortDirection=none&newquery=Disability+Employment&content-type=Reference+table&contenttype=Dataset

6. The Annual Population Survey March 2013, retrieved from NOMIS: www.nomisweb.co.uk

7. The Annual Population Survey March 2013, retrieved from NOMIS: www.nomisweb.co.uk

8. Office for National Statistics, 2014, Life Opportunities Survey: Wave 2, Part 2 results, (online), available at: https://www.gov.uk/government/statistics/life-opportunitiessurvey-wave-2-part-2-results

9. Office for Disability Issues, 2011, ODI Life Opportunities Survey Wave One results, p10 (online), available at: https://www.gov.uk/government/statistics/life-opportunitiessurvey-wave-one-results-2009-to-2011

10. Office for Disability Issues, 2012, Measuring National Well-being – Education and Skills, p.26, (online), available at: http://www.ons.gov.uk/ons dcp171766_268091.pdf

11. Office for National Statistics, 2014, Life Opportunities Survey: Wave 2, Part 2 results, (online), available at: https://www.gov.uk/government/statistics/life-opportunitiessurvey-wave-2-part-2-results

12. Department for Work and Pensions, 2014, Households Below Average Income, (online), available at: https:// www.gov.uk/government/uploads/ system/uploads/attachment_data/file/325416/households-below-averageincome-1994-1995-2012-2013.pdf

13. Department for Work and Pensions, 2014, Households Below Average Income, (online), available at: https://www.gov.uk/government/uploads/system/uploads/attachment_data/file/325416/households-below-averageincome-1994-1995-2012-2013.pdf .

14. Department for Work and Pensions, 2014, Households Below Average Income, (online), available at: https://www.gov.uk/government/uploads/system/uploads/attachment_data/file/325416/households-below-averageincome-1994-1995-2012-2013.pdf

disabled people are in low-income households.[15]

⇨ Disabled people pay on average £550 per month on extra costs related to their disability. As a result of these extra costs, disabled people are twice as likely to have unsecured debt totalling more than half of their household income.[16]

⇨ Disabled men experience a pay gap of 11% compared with non-disabled men, while the gap between disabled women and non-disabled women is double this at 22%.[17]

⇨ Disabled people experience much lower economic living standards than their peers.[18]

⇨ Disabled people face a disproportionate likelihood of living in a deprived area, and are more likely than non-disabled people to live in poor housing.[19]

⇨ There is a shortage of housing that is specifically designed to meet disabled people's needs.[20]

⇨ The majority of homes in England (84%) do not allow someone using a wheelchair to get to and through the front door without difficulty.[21]

⇨ Transport is the largest concern for disabled people in their local area. Pavement/road maintenance, access, and frequency of public transport are the biggest issues.[22]

⇨ It is estimated there are 62,000 disability motivated hate crimes each year.[23]

⇨ The annual cost of bringing up a disabled child is three times greater than that of bringing up a non disabled child.[24]

⇨ 40% of disabled children in the UK live in poverty. This accounts for around 320,000 disabled children, and almost a third of those are classified as living in "severe poverty".[25]

⇨ Children in families containing one or more disabled person are twice as likely to live in households with combined low income and material deprivation as those in families with no disabled person (22% compared to 10%).[26]

⇨ One in four people will experience mental ill health in any given year.[27]

⇨ Overall, one in ten adults in Britain experience depression at any one time. Around one in 20 people at any one time experience major or 'clinical' depression.[28]

⇨ Nearly four in ten people thought of disabled people as less productive than non-disabled people, and 75% of people thought of disabled people as needing to be cared for some or most of the time. This suggests a degree of 'benevolent prejudice' exists towards disabled people.[29]

⇨ It is estimated that the number of older disabled people is likely to increase by around 40% between 2002 and 2022, if age-related disability rates remain constant.[30]

⇨ The World Health Organization has predicted that depression will be the leading cause of disability by 2020. Mental ill health and learning disabilities in particular are anticipated to grow.[31]

⇨ Disabled people are disadvantaged in the labour market in all European countries. At the European Union (EU) level, about 47% of disabled people are employed, compared to

15. The Poverty Site, Key Facts, (online), available at: http://www.poverty.org.uk/summary/key%20facts.shtml#disability (Accessed

16. Scope, 2014, Priced Out: ending the financial penalty of disability by 2020, p6, (online), available at: http://www. scope.org.uk/Scope/media/Images/ Publication%20Directory/Priced-out. pdf?ext=.pdf

17. Equality and Human Rights Commission, 2010, How fair is Britain? The first Triennial Review Executive Survey, (online), available at: http://www.equalityhumanrights. com/uploaded_files/triennial_review/tr_ execsumm.pd

18. Equality and Human Rights Commission, 2010, 'How fair is Britain?', (online), available at: http://www.equalityhumanrights.com/sites/ default/files/documents/triennial_review/ tr_execsumm.pdf

19. Department for Communities and Local Government, 2009, English House Condition Survey 2007, (online), available at: http://www. esds.ac.uk/doc/6449/mrdoc/pdf/6449ehcs_ annual_report_2007.pdf

20. Department for Communities and Local Government, 2009, English House Condition Survey 2007, (online), available at: http://www. esds.ac.uk/doc/6449/mrdoc/pdf/6449ehcs_ annual_report_2007.pdf

21. Habinteg, Mind the Step: An estimation of housing needs among wheelchair users in England, p5, (online), available at: http://www.habinteg.org.uk/mediaFiles/ downloads/94842268/Mind_the_step_ onlineversion_pdf.pdf

22. Transport Research and Innovation Portal (TRIP), 08/2001 - 03/2003, Attitudes of Disabled People to Public Transport, available at: http://www.transportresearch. info/web/projects/project_details. cfm?id=7441&page=contact

23. Home Office, 2014, Hate crimes, England and Wales 2013 to 2014, (online), available at: https://www.gov.uk/government/statistics/ hate-crimes-england-and-wales2013-to-2014

24. Contact a Family, 2012. Counting the Costs 2012 The financial reality for families with disabled children across the UK, (online), available at: http://www.cafamily.org. uk/media/381221/counting_the_costs_2012_ full_report.pdf

25. The Children's Society, 2011, 4 in every 10: Disabled children living in poverty, (online), available at: http://www.childrenssociety. org.uk/sites/default/files/tcs/4_in_10reportfinal. pdf

26. Department for Work and Pensions, 2014, Households Below Average Income, p85, (online), available at: https://www.gov. uk/government/uploads/system/uploads/ attachment_data/file/325416/households- below-averageincome-1994-1995-2012-2013. pdf

27. Mind, 2009, Facts and Statistics about Mental Health, (online), available at: http://www.mind.org.uk/informationsupport/ types-of-mental-health-problems/statistics- and-facts-about-mental-health/how-common- are-mental-health problems/

28. Mind, Facts and Statistics about Mental Health, (online), available at: http://www. mind.org.uk/mental_health_az/8105_mental_ health_facts_and_statistics

29. Office for Disability Issues, 2011, Public Perceptions of Disabled People: Evidence from the British Social Attitudes Survey 2009, p.9, (online), available at: https://www.gov. uk/government/uploads/system/uploads/ attachment_data/file/325989/ppdp.pdf

30. Institute for Public Policy Research (IPPR), 2007, Disability 2020: Opportunities for the full and equal citizenship of disabled people in Britain in 2020, p11, (online), available at: http://www.ippr.org/assets/media/ images/media/files/publication/2011/05/ Disability_2020_full_1568.pdf

31. Institute for Public Policy Research (IPPR), 2007, Disability 2020: Opportunities for the full and equal citizenship of disabled people in Britain in 2020, p8, (online), available at: http://www.ippr.org/assets/media/ images/media/files/publication/2011/05/ Disability_2020_full_1568.pdf

- 72% of non-disabled people. The average employment gap is 25%.[32]

- Disabled people face a higher risk of poverty compared to non-disabled people across all EU member states. At the EU level, 19% of disabled people face the risk of living in poverty, compared to 15% of non-disabled people.[33]

- People in nursing/care/retirement establishments and long-stay hospitals are not included in these figures.

- The above extract is reprinted with kind permission from The Papworth Trust. For further information please visit www.papworthtrust.org.uk for further information.

© 2018 Papworth Trust

32. Academic Network of European Disability Experts (ANED), 2013, European comparative data on Europe 2020 and people with disabilities, (online), available at: http://www.disability-europe.net/theme/comparative-data/reports-comparativedata

33. Academic Network of European Disability Experts (ANED), 2013, European comparative data on Europe 2020 and people with disabilities, (online), available at: http://www.disability-europe.net/theme/comparative-data/reports-comparativedata

Autism spectrum disorder (ASD)

Overview

Autism spectrum disorder (ASD) is the name for a range of similar conditions, including Asperger syndrome, that affect a person's social interaction, communication, interests and behaviour.

In children with ASD, the symptoms are present before three years of age, although a diagnosis can sometimes be made after the age of three.

It's estimated that about one in every 100 people in the UK has ASD. More boys are diagnosed with the condition than girls.

There's no 'cure' for ASD, but speech and language therapy, occupational therapy, educational support, plus a number of other interventions are available to help children and parents.

Read about help and support available for people with ASD.

Signs and symptoms

People with ASD tend to have problems with social interaction and communication.

In early infancy, some children with ASD don't babble or use other vocal sounds. Older children have problems using non-verbal behaviours to interact with others – for example, they have difficulty with eye contact, facial expressions, body language and gestures. They may give no or brief eye contact and ignore familiar or unfamiliar people.

Children with ASD may also lack awareness of and interest in other children. They'll often either gravitate to older or younger children, rather than interacting with children of the same age. They tend to play alone.

They can find it hard to understand other people's emotions and feelings, and have difficulty starting conversations or taking part in them properly. Language development may be delayed, and a child with ASD won't compensate their lack of language or delayed language skills by using gestures (body language) or facial expressions.

Children with ASD will tend to repeat words or phrases spoken by others (either immediately or later) without formulating their own language, or in parallel to developing their language skills. Some children don't demonstrate imaginative or pretend play, while others will continually repeat the same pretend play.

Some children with ASD like to stick to the same routine and little changes may trigger tantrums. Some children may flap their hand or twist or flick their fingers when they're excited or upset. Others may engage in repetitive activity, such as turning light switches on and off, opening and closing doors, or lining things up.

Children and young people with ASD frequently experience a range of cognitive (thinking), learning, emotional and behavioural problems. For example, they may also have attention deficit hyperactivity disorder (ADHD), anxiety, or depression.

About 70% of children with ASD have a non-verbal IQ below 70. Of these, 50% have a non-verbal IQ below 50. Overall, up to 50% of people with severe learning difficulties have an ASD.

Getting a diagnosis

The main features of ASD – problems with social communication and interaction – can often be recognised during early childhood.

Some features of ASD may not become noticeable until a change of situation, such as when the child starts nursery or school.

See your GP or health visitor if you notice any of the signs and symptoms of ASD in your child, or if you're concerned about your child's development. It can also be helpful to discuss your concerns with your child's nursery or school.

Caring for someone with ASD

Being a carer isn't an easy role. When you're busy responding to the needs of others, it can affect your emotional and physical energy, and make it easy to forget your own health and mental wellbeing.

If you're caring for someone else, it's important to look after yourself and get as much help as possible. It's in your best interests and those of the person you care for.

What causes ASD?

The exact cause of ASD is unknown, but it's thought that several complex genetic and environmental factors are involved.

In the past, some people believed the MMR vaccine caused ASD, but this has been investigated extensively in a number of major studies around the world, involving millions of children, and researchers have found no evidence of a link between MMR and ASD.

Autism in adults

Some people with ASD had features of the condition as a child, but enter adulthood without ever being diagnosed.

However, getting a diagnosis as an adult can often help a person with ASD and their families understand the condition, and work out what type of advice and support they need.

For example, a number of autism-specific services are available that provide adults with ASD with the help and support they need to live independently and find a job that matches their skills and abilities.

⇨ The above extract is reprinted with kind permission from NHS Choices. Please visit www.nhs.uk for further information.

© NHS Choices 2018

The things every child with autism wishes you knew

An article from The Conversation.

Helen Driver, PhD Researcher in Autism, Family and Communication, Northumbria University, Newcastle and Joanna Reynolds, Research Psychologist and Senior Lecturer in Child and Family Wellbeing, Northumbria University, Newcastle

We are often quick to make judgements on what we perceive to be happening when children behave in a way that draws attention – but when a young person with autism is struggling to cope with the world, the last thing they need is our criticism.

"These ten tips reflect our combined experience of research and close engagement with children with autism. And as a proud parent of a boy with autism, I would like everyone to think more about how they respond to children"

Because if we take time to respect and understand people with autism our communities will become more enriching and inclusive for everyone.

1. See me for who I am

There is only one of me, just like there is only one of you in the world. Like you, I have lots of different skills and abilities as well as things I find difficult. Just because I have autism doesn't mean I am the same as everyone else with autism. Love and acceptance from family, friends and everyone around me is the best way to help me to grow and thrive.

2. I hear, see and feel the world differently to you

I find some noises, smells, tastes or lights stressful, frightening or even physically painful. Touch can overwhelm me and I might not like hugs. But I can experience details that you might miss – that I can enjoy and find funny or exciting – so come and share these things with me. Read some of the books written by people with autism to learn more about how the world can feel.

3. I want friends, just like everyone else

But my social behaviour might seem different from other people's. For me, communication and interaction isn't just through words. Some children with autism don't use spoken language and communicate in non-verbal ways. This can include taking your hand to the object I want, or looking at something of interest – so watch me and learn my language.

4. My behaviour is my way of communicating

If I can't talk or express my thoughts and feelings I can become very frustrated, sad and angry. People see my behaviour as difficult, naughty or deliberately challenging – but it's likely to be my way of communicating. Don't exacerbate these outbursts, help me say what I want to.

5. Interact with me in ways I can understand

Slow down and give me time. Be clear about what you say, and give me the chance to react – it takes up to ten to 15 seconds for me to process what you say. Get to know my interests and my ways of communicating. And let my interests inspire your communication with me. Don't try to take over or control our interaction. Give me space and time to respond. When you learn to listen with all your senses you'll realise how much I have to say.

6. I live in the here and now

I don't always understand the bigger picture so understanding things in context may be difficult for me. Show me pictures and let me know what to expect and I can join in so much more easily.

7. I am anxious and worry a lot

This is because I have difficulties understanding the world and communicating my thoughts and needs. The way I see, hear or feel the world can be painful, and the world can be a frightening and confusing place for me. When something happens or changes suddenly, I may panic. People might think I'm being silly but I am really terrified.

8. Routine is really important to me

Because it makes me feel safe and helps me to cope. That doesn't mean I don't want to experience new things. I just need more support to join in with the world. If you help me, I can find activities and sports that I will enjoy and you can enjoy with me. Find out what helps to calm me. If I am less anxious I can cope with more.

9. I need your help to access the world and learn

Every child with autism can learn. You just need to take time to understand how I make sense of the world and make learning relevant to me. Everyone learns in different ways. I might need to move more and use visual resources but I love to achieve and learn – it's a great way to help me feel more confident.

10. Think about what I can do, not what I can't

I am a clever, sociable, whole person. I may be more interested in certain specific subjects and pick up on the detail more, but this is my interest. My brother may spend hours watching and playing football, my friend might like aliens, and I like talking about my videos and finding out people's names. Love me and work with me and enjoy what I bring to the world.

4 April 2017

⇨ The above information is reprinted with kind permission from *The Conversation*. Please visit www.theconversation.com for further information.

Down's syndrome

An extract from an article by NHS Choices.

Overview

Down's syndrome, also known as Down syndrome or trisomy 21, is a genetic condition that typically causes some level of learning disability and certain physical characteristics.

Characteristics of Down's syndrome

Most babies born with Down's syndrome are diagnosed soon after birth and may have:

⇨ floppiness (hypotonia)

⇨ eyes that slant upwards and outwards

⇨ a small mouth with a tongue that may stick out

⇨ a flat back of the head

⇨ below-average weight and length at birth

⇨ their palm may have only one crease across it.

Although children with Down's syndrome share some common physical characteristics, they don't all look the same. A child with Down's will look more like their family members than other children who have the syndrome.

People with Down's syndrome will also have different personalities and abilities. Everyone born with Down's syndrome will have some degree of learning disability, but this will be different for each person.

Screening for Down's syndrome

Sometimes parents find out their baby has Down's syndrome during pregnancy because of screening tests. All pregnant women are offered screening tests for Down's syndrome.

Screening tests can't tell you for certain if your baby has Down's syndrome, but they can tell you how likely it is.

If screening tests show there's a chance your baby has Down's, more tests can be done during pregnancy to confirm it.

These include:

⇨ **chorionic villus sampling (CVS)** – a small sample of the placenta is tested, usually during weeks 11–14 of pregnancy

⇨ **amniocentesis** – a sample of amniotic fluid is tested, usually during weeks 15–20 of pregnancy

Causes of Down's syndrome

Down's syndrome is usually caused by an extra chromosome in a baby's cells. In most cases, this isn't inherited – it's simply the result of a one-off genetic change in the sperm or egg.

There's a small chance of having a child with Down's syndrome with any pregnancy, but the likelihood increases with the age of the mother.

For example, a woman who is 20 has about a one in 1,500 chance of having a baby with Down's, while a woman who is 40 has a one in 100 chance.

There's no evidence that anything done before or during pregnancy increases or decreases the chance of having a child with Down's syndrome.

Living with Down's syndrome

Although there's no 'cure' for Down's syndrome, there's support available to help children with the condition lead healthy, fulfilling lives.

This includes:

⇨ access to good healthcare – including a range of different specialists

⇨ support for your child's development – this may include speech and language therapy, physiotherapy, and home teaching

⇨ support groups – such as the Down's Syndrome Association, who can put you in touch with other families who have a child with Down's syndrome.

Lots of people with Down's syndrome are able to leave home, have relationships, work, and lead largely independent lives.

Health problems linked to Down's syndrome

People with Down's syndrome are more likely to have certain health problems, including:

⇨ heart disorders, such as congenital heart disease

⇨ hearing and vision problems

⇨ thyroid problems, such as an underactive thyroid gland (hypothyroidism)

⇨ recurrent infections, such as pneumonia.

30 April 2017

⇨ The above information is reprinted with kind permission from NHS Choices. Please visit www.nhs.uk for further information.

Dyspraxia at a glance... what is dyspraxia?

Movement Matters, an umbrella organisation representing major national groups in the UK that represent people with coordination difficulties offers the following definition:

Developmental Coordination Disorder (DCD), also known as dyspraxia, is a common disorder affecting fine and/or gross motor coordination in children and adults. DCD is formally recognised by international organisations including the World Health Organization. DCD is distinct from other motor disorders such as cerebral palsy and stroke, and occurs across the range of intellectual abilities. Individuals may vary in how their difficulties present: these may change over time depending on environmental demands and life experiences, and will persist into adulthood.

An individual's coordination difficulties may affect participation and functioning of everyday life skills in education, work and employment. Children may present with difficulties with self-care, writing, typing, riding a bike and play as well as other educational and recreational activities. In adulthood many of these difficulties will continue, as well as learning new skills at home, in education and work, such as driving a car and DIY. There may be a range of co-occurring difficulties which can also have serious negative impacts on daily life. These include social and emotional difficulties as well as problems with time management, planning and personal organisation, and these may also affect an adult's education or employment experiences.

The Dyspraxia Foundation adds to the Movement Matters description, recognising the many non-motor difficulties that may also be experienced by people with the condition and which can have a significant impact on daily life activities. These include memory, perception and processing as well as additional problems with planning, organising and carrying out movements in the right order in everyday situations. Although dyspraxia may occur in isolation, it frequently coexists with other conditions such as Attention Deficit Hyperactive Disorder (ADHD), dyslexia, language disorders and social, emotional and behavioural impairments.

The Dyspraxia Foundation also provides support to people affected by verbal dyspraxia (also known as 'childhood apraxia of speech'), which can occur alongside motor coordination difficulties, or as a separate condition. A definition and information about verbal dyspraxia is provided separately.

What causes dyspraxia?

For the majority of those with the condition, there is no known cause. Current research suggests that it is due to an immaturity of neurone development in the brain rather than to brain damage. People with dyspraxia have no clinical neurological abnormality to explain their condition.

How would I recognise a child with dyspraxia?

The pre-school child

⇨ Is late in reaching milestones, e.g. rolling over, sitting, standing, walking and speaking

⇨ May not be able to run, hop, jump, or catch or kick a ball although their peers can do so

⇨ Has difficulty in keeping friends; or judging how to behave in company

⇨ Has little understanding of concepts such as 'in', 'on', 'in front of', etc.

⇨ Has difficulty in walking up and down stairs

⇨ Poor at dressing

⇨ Slow and hesitant in most actions

⇨ Appears not to be able to learn anything instinctively but must be taught skills

⇨ Falls over frequently

⇨ Poor pencil grip

⇨ Cannot do jigsaws or shape sorting games

⇨ Artwork is very immature

⇨ Often anxious and easily distracted.

The school age child

⇨ Probably has all the difficulties experienced by the pre-school child with dyspraxia, with little or no improvement

⇨ Avoids PE and games

⇨ Does badly in class but significantly better on a one-to-one basis

⇨ Reacts to all stimuli without discrimination and attention span is poor

⇨ May have trouble with maths and writing structured stories

⇨ Experiences great difficulty in copying from the blackboard

⇨ Writes laboriously and immaturely

⇨ Unable to remember and/or follow instructions

⇨ Is generally poorly organised.

⇨ The above information is reprinted with kind permission from the Dyspraxia Foundation. Please visit www.dyspraxiafoundation.org.uk for further information.

© 2018 Dyspraxia Foundation

Mapping Disability | our findings

Almost

1 in 5

people in England have a long standing limiting disability or illness.

Almost

70%

of disabled people are aged over 50.

Over

50%

of disabled people state that they experience long-term pain.

Almost

50%

of disabled people have a long-term health condition.

There are slightly more disabled females than males in England.

Almost

75%

of disabled people have more than one impairment.

SPORT ENGLAND

Survey reveals enormous hidden impact of arthritis on mental wellbeing

A survey released by Arthritis Care (Tuesday 9 May) reveals the enormous hidden impact that living with arthritis is having on mental wellbeing.

More than 3,000 people with arthritis responded to the charity's survey from across the UK and of those, 79% (four out of five) said their condition made them feel anxious or depressed.

Arthritis affects one-fifth of adults in the UK, that's ten million people living with arthritis.

The charity is sharing the survey findings in Arthritis Care Week (8–14 May) to launch **Wake up to Arthritis**, a new campaign to raise awareness of the seriousness of arthritis.

Key survey findings:

⇨ 79% (four in five) feel anxious or depressed because of their arthritis

⇨ 80% (four in five) have given up activities they enjoy

⇨ Half (50%) feel isolated or lonely because of their arthritis, with 47% having lost contact with friends

⇨ Only 43% felt able to manage their arthritis well

⇨ 58% struggle with daily activities like washing, dressing or making meals

⇨ 89% worry about how arthritis will affect their future independence.

The survey shows that feelings of anxiety and depression are more common among those who experience severe pain and fatigue, who struggle with daily activities, and who have lost contact with friends or given up activities they enjoy.

Arthritis Care is calling for real change for people with arthritis, including:

⇨ Better recognition of the impact of arthritis by governments and health services across the UK

⇨ Better integration of mental and physical health services

⇨ Better access to support with self-management and pain management services.

9 May 2017

⇨ The above information is reprinted with kind permission from Arthritis Care. Please visit www.arthritiscare.org.uk for further information.

Without European intervention, equality for disabled people in Britain would be a distant dream

An article from **The Conversation.**

THE CONVERSATION

Paul Chaney, Professor of Policy and Politics, Cardiff University

The representation of disabled people in government has never been more important. In 2014, 19% of British residents said that they were disabled. The country also has an ageing population and 42% of state pension age adults – five million people altogether – are living with disabilities.

Before the EU referendum, fears abound that the laws in place to help and protect the lives of disabled people would be disregarded, and future progress stilted. We have yet to see what impact Brexit will have, but my own research has revealed one extremely concerning fact: parliament is, and has been for some time, filled with institutionalised ableism, and without the EU's help, the situation for disabled people may become very dire indeed.

Low priority

Even at the very start of policy and law development, disability is a very low priority. Looking just at early day motions (EDMs) – which allows MPs to voice their opinions on certain issues with no expectation to toe the party line – disability ranks behind gender and age among the protected characteristics that will get attention from lawmakers.

The motions give a good insight into MPs' priorities. For example, Chris Ruane, former MP for the Vale of Clwyd, in 2009 specifically demanded "that this house notes... heart disease, diabetes, stroke and kidney disease, remain the number one cause of disability in the UK... and calls on the Government to work with the voluntary sector... to ensure that the best care is available to those people affected".

Though there was some increase in the number of EDMs that were proposed for the benefit of "disabled peoples", the rate of change has been slow. When you compare the number of disability/disabled people's EDMs in the 1992–97 parliament with the 2005–10 parliament the growth is negligible – just 3.5 percentage points.

It's clear just from these motions that disability issues are far from a mainstream policy priority for most MPs. Even though each constituency would have a significant number of disabled people, less than a third of MPs put forward a specific disability EDM between 1990 and 2012.

There are also big differences in each political party's record of proposing disability/disabled people EDMs. Almost two-thirds of the total proposed between 1990 and 2012 were tabled by Labour Party backbenchers. Liberal Democrat MPs put forward just under a quarter, while Conservative MPs accounted for less than 10%. The rest were put forward by "others" such as the Scottish National Party, and Plaid Cymru.

Looking at how these motions were framed, most were concerned with securing a decent level of living for disabled people, followed by tackling discrimination, and raising awareness of disabled people's rights. When broken down by policy area the lead topics were taxation, pensions and social security (just over a quarter of the total); health (just over a fifth); transport; employment; and education. The lead topic here points to the economic marginalisation and poverty experienced by disabled people. The others indicate that the associated problems disabled people experience span all areas of social welfare.

Institutionalised ableism

This research is more than just stats. It confirms a clear history of marginalisation and representational failings reaching back as far as World War II. Until 1970, there were just four main laws put in place that were concerned with disability. This marginalisation continued through to the 1990s when a small number of statutes were passed – though it must be noted that these were landmark pieces of legislation, such as the 1995 Disability Discrimination Act, for example.

Overall, disabled people's representation is far from a mainstream issue in Westminster law-making. In fact it would be fair to say that without European intervention from the EU and European Convention on Human Rights, equality for disabled people would still be falling behind.

The 2010 Equality Act, the UN Convention on the Rights of Persons with Disabilities (ratified by the UK in 2009) and EC Directives on equality require the promotion of equality for disabled people in the exercise of public functions – including parliamentary representation, policy and law-making. It is in this context that Brexit is revealed as a wholly negative development for disabled people.

European legislation has been a key driver of equality for disabled people and others with protected characteristics in the UK. Going forward, vigilance will be an absolute necessity to ensure there is no reduction in disabled people's rights and protections when the UK leaves the EU, and the Conservative Government moves forward with replacing the European Convention of Human Rights with a domestic bill of rights.

Disability rights campaigners, already a strong voice, will have their work cut out for them going forward. Meanwhile MPs will need to sit up and realise that these rights must be safeguarded. Discrimination cannot continue.

13 March 2017

⇨ The above information is reprinted with kind permission from *The Conversation*. Please visit www.theconversation.com for further information.

Reactive, not proactive: Update on the lack of disabled toilets on UK trains

By Josephine Nwaamaka Bardi

Having recently raised the issue of a lack of disabled toilets on a UK train service, Josephine reflects on the recent media coverage resulting from the experience of paralympian, Anne Wafula-Strike, having no access to a toilet throughout a train journey.

A few weeks after my blog on the lack of disabled toilets on an East Midlands train was published, the media has been bombarding the public with Anne Wafula-Strike (MBE)'s experience on a CrossCountry train that did not have a functional disabled toilet.

I empathise with Anne, but I hate to think that it had to take a celebrity and well-known public figure for the Government or the press to acknowledge the lack of accessible disabled toilets on UK trains. Whatever happened to efficient service provision for a service that was paid for? Disabled or not, famous or not, amenities on trains should be in working order for all.

What a coincidence one might say, my blog was published on 8 December,

the same day that Anne travelled on the CrossCountry train. Although something tells me that there is a likelihood that many more people have had similar experiences to Anne, but they did not tell anyone and the press failed to pick it up or ignored them.

According to Anne, "by the time they reached a station with a disabled toilet, it was too late". The good thing about this is that it may not be too late for other disabled persons who travel on trains in the future… Then again, who knows what excuses the train managing directors will ask us to understand, such as this ridiculous one: "trains hitting cows" (Andy Cooper, Managing Director of CrossCountry).

I remember once having to pay double the cost of travel because my train from Eltham to St Pancras was delayed and the time when I forgot my rail card so had to pay more. I would really like someone at the train office to understand that those excuses were true.

Now on the issue of train companies ignoring complaints about the lack of or faulty disabled toilets on trains, Anne stated that Andy Cooper added that Anne would be offered "complimentary first-class travel tickets by way of an apology". At least CrossCountry trains bothered to respond and apologise. *Nursing Times* contacted East Midlands trains for their comment before my blog on the lack of functional disabled toilets on their train was published, their response arrived almost two months later.

In their 3 January article, *The Guardian* asked people with disabilities to write to them about their inadequate services for disabled people. OK, don't get me wrong, I may not be considered disabled, but I am a mental health nurse who cares about health and wellbeing and I feel that we need a more proactive, rather than this reactive, response to this sort of health issue.

The Independent, BBC, *Guardian* and now the rail minister, Paul Maynard, have decided to act. But why did it have to take this type of situation for anyone to notice that such an important aspect of service provision was missing from an industry that charges travellers very high prices for train journeys?

12 January 2017

⇨ This article was originally published on www.nursingtimes. net and is reproduced with kind permission of Emap Publishing Ltd. Please visit www. nursingtimes.net for further information.

Premier League clubs face legal threat unless disabled access is improved

EHRC chair David Isaacs says the time for excuses from the clubs is over.

13 of 20 top-flight teams do not have required wheelchair spaces

Premier League clubs' failure to provide minimum levels of access for disabled supporters has been described as "disappointing" by the Equality and Human Rights Commission (EHRC), which has again threatened legal action if they do not comply.

The warning followed a Premier League report which revealed that 13 of its 20 clubs' grounds do not incorporate the minimum number of wheelchair spaces set out in the accessible stadia guide (ASG) and that nine of the clubs will not make the necessary improvements in time for the league's own self-imposed deadline of this August.

David Isaac, EHRC chair, responded in an uncompromising statement: "[The] Premier League promised that disabled access would be improved by the start of next season, so it is disappointing that a number of clubs will fail to meet that deadline. The time for excuses is over. Clubs need to urgently demonstrate to us what they are doing to ensure they are compliant with the law and how they are making it easier for disabled fans to attend matches. If they don't, they will face legal action."

The ASG provides official guidance for sports clubs on the disability access needed to comply with the Equality Act 2010, which requires organisations to make "reasonable adjustments" for disabled people so that they can enjoy the same quality of experience as non-disabled people. Following years of campaigning by disabled supporters and groups led by the organisation Level Playing Field, and the first threats of legal action by the EHRC from March 2015, the Premier League pledged in September 2015 that its clubs would comply with the ASG by the start of the 2017–18 season. Earlier this month a critical report by the parliamentary committee for culture, media and sport said it would support legal action if the clubs fail to meet the pledge.

The detailed progress report on the work being undertaken by all 20 clubs notes that most of those currently not providing the minimum number of wheelchair spaces or recommended facilities have appointed architects to consider how to comply. However, only four of the 13 which fall short – Liverpool, Stoke, Sunderland and West Bromwich Albion – are planning to make the necessary improvements, which usually involve significant building work and displacement of seats, by the August deadline.

Tottenham Hotspur, who will move to Wembley next season, say their new stadium at White Hart Lane will be fully compliant with the ASG when it opens for the 2018–19 season. Chelsea pledge to incorporate full disability access to the new 60,000-seat stadium at Stamford Bridge for which the club was recently given planning permission and say they are seeking to address the significant current shortfall of wheelchair spaces in the short term.

The clubs promoted last season whose stadiums do not comply, Hull City and Burnley – Middlesbrough say their Riverside stadium does – have been given a further year to make the necessary improvements.

Arsenal, Everton, Leicester City and Manchester United have pledged to carry out the necessary works and improve their facilities for disabled supporters, but not by the deadline of August this year. Watford, whose Vicarage Road ground has 61 wheelchair spaces, substantially short of the ASG recommended 153, have issued a detailed public statement setting out that 31 more spaces are to be built by August, and more phased in over time. The club and its disabled supporters group WFC Enables have said the new total of 92 will exceed current demand.

Clubs are facing challenges of planning, construction and the disruption to other supporters, the league said in a statement, saying of the planned work: "It is almost certainly the largest and most ambitious set of improvements in disabled access undertaken by any group of sport or entertainment venues in the UK."

The Premier League said its clubs had come to a recognition that "more could be done" to welcome disabled supporters to its grounds and said "cost is not a determining factor" in the difficulties of complying.

Tony Taylor, the chair of LPF, said in response: "We do recognise that a lot of work is going on and we have made incredible progress in the last few years. However, it has been a long time coming, these levels of provision for disabled supporters are just a minimum legal requirement and we expect all clubs to comply as quickly as possible."

1 February 2017

⇨ The above information is reprinted with kind permission from *The Guardian*. Please visit www.theguardian.com for further information.

Accessibility of Sports Stadia contents

An extract from an article by parliament UK.

1. It is very clear that sports clubs, notably many of those with very considerable income and resources, have not given priority to sports fans with disabilities in recent years, despite the increase in income many of those clubs have received.

The experiences of those with disabilities

2. Disabled spectators are not asking for a large number of expensive changes. They love their sports and wish only for their needs to be taken into account in the way sports stadia are designed and operated. As we go on to describe, a number of clubs are already providing disabled supporters with a good experience when they attend matches, and more could do so. It is high time that sports clubs, particularly those with available finance such as those in football's Premier League, changed their mindset. It is more a question of will than resources.

The response to date

3. Consideration should be given to devising a confidential reporting regime to enable complaints to be made without adverse consequences for those who complain.

4. We expect the needs of disabled fans to receive priority over the desire to charge a premium for extra hospitality accommodation.

5. There is plenty of guidance available as to what adjustments might be considered reasonable for sports grounds (listed, for example, in Annex A of *The Inclusive and Accessible Stadia Report*) and many of the obvious ways to ameliorate the problems described above do not require considerable capital or disruption to the stadia and those visiting. Disability awareness training, professional access audits and design appraisals are not expensive and are available from a number of organisations. The start-up cost of a full Audio Descriptive Commentary Service is only £4,000 per club. While the provision of extra wheelchair spaces, adequate lifts and more disabled toilets may require substantial building work, many clubs have made, are making or are planning major building works in which these might be included.

6. We strongly applaud the work done by a number of football clubs in meeting both the letter and the spirit of the Disability Discrimination Act. We accept that other sports have made less progress to date, but we note Level Playing Field's belief that rugby league, rugby union and county cricket clubs are taking the issue seriously. We encourage these sports to persist. However, we consider it completely unacceptable that a number of Premier League clubs – some of the richest sporting organisations in the UK – have failed to carry out even basic adaptations in over 20 years. Given the huge public investment in converting the Olympic Stadium into a Premier League football ground, we would expect all the partners involved to ensure that West Ham, at the very least, becomes an exemplar regarding disabled access.

7. We concur with Ministers that it is in the sports' own interests to pay more attention to the – often very moderate – needs of such a large proportion of the UK population. Most clubs do not sell all the tickets for games, and a reputation for being well adapted and welcoming to disabled supporters should enhance their reputations generally. Conversely, it could be considered a reputational risk – and one which sponsors would have to take seriously – if clubs continued to fail to engage with

reasonable adjustments and thereby be in breach of the law.

8. The Premier League told us that it would consider imposing sanctions on clubs that fail to provide sufficient accessibility. However, it is not clear whether this relates only to the physical modifications that should be made to stadia, rather than the broader view of the quality of the overall experience for supporters with disabilities. Given 20 years of comparative inactivity by the football leagues, we are not convinced that the Premier League would impose suitable penalties on clubs, even for failing to meet building regulations.

9. The Equality and Human Rights Commission has told us that it is minded to start legal proceedings against clubs that continue to flout the law. We support them in this action.

13 January 2017

⇨ The above extract is reprinted with kind permission from Parliament UK. Please visit www. publications.parliament.uk for further information.

© Crown copyright 2018

Disabled passengers win partial Supreme Court victory in battle for priority use of bus wheelchair space

The case was triggered when a disabled man was left at the stop because a woman with a baby in a pushchair refused to move out of the designated area when asked by the bus driver.

By Mary Bulman

Disabled travellers have won a partial victory at the Supreme Court in their battle for priority use of wheelchair spaces on buses.

The case was triggered when a wheelchair user from West Yorkshire attempted to board a bus operated by FirstGroup, which had a sign saying: "Please give up this space if needed for a wheelchair user".

Doug Paulley was left at the stop because a woman with a sleeping baby in a pushchair refused to move out of the designated area when asked by the bus driver, saying the buggy would not fold.

FirstGroup has a policy of "requesting but not requiring" non-disabled travellers, including those with babies and pushchairs, to vacate the space if it is needed by a wheelchair user.

Following the incident, a judge at Leeds County Court ruled that bus companies were not legally required to compel parents to move their children's buggies to make way for wheelchair users, and that the "proper remedy" for wheelchair users to get

improvements in such cases is to ask parliament.

But a judge at Leeds County Court has now ruled that the policy breached FirstGroup's duty under the Equality Act 2010 to make "reasonable adjustments" for disabled people.

Lord Neuberger, the Supreme Court's president, explained that Mr Paulley's appeal was being allowed, but only to the limited extent that FirstGroup's policy requiring a driver to simply request a non-wheelchair user to vacate the space without taking any further steps was unjustified.

18 January 2017

⇨ The above information is reprinted with kind permission from *The Independent*. Please visit www. independent.co.uk for further information.

© independent.co.uk 2018

Using augmented reality to help disabled shoppers

By Adi Gaskell

Augmented reality has become increasingly powerful in the past year as the technology gradually moves from gimmick status to something more worthwhile. One of the more interesting applications attempts to make the shopping experience more friendly for disabled shoppers.

This is a particular issue, as the shopping experience is not generally designed with disabled people in mind, and research suggests that many dislike asking for assistance when shopping. Getting help from technology however was different, so the researchers set about designing just that.

Augmented shopping

They set about developing a pilot that utilized augmented reality to help people with three different levels of impairment.

The team developed an app for the first group and tested it in a dummy store setup. When the consumer entered the store, they loaded the app and it presented them with a virtual replica of the store. When the consumer came upon something they liked in the store, they pointed their device at it. The shelves, which were equipped with augmented reality, then communicated their contents to the device.

The information on the app was updated in real time, complete with information such as price and expiry date. As soon as the shoppers had filled their virtual baskets and were ready to check out, staff would collect each item for them, and process them.

When the test subjects were quizzed after the experiment, they revealed they felt more independent than they normally would when shopping. It was an experience more akin to that of online shopping, but in the real world.

"These interfaces are helpful to me to do shopping by myself without asking or requiring the assistance of other people. I would like to have it available at real shops, and think that getting used to something like this is very easy, and it is an opportunity to be more independent," one participant said.

Suffice to say, a system like this is some way from entering the market, let alone the mainstream, with the kind of smart shelves used in the study considerably more expensive than existing systems. There are positive signs however, with many retailers beginning to install such shelving to help them with both stock control and theft prevention. If such an infrastructure begins to exist, then piggybacking such a system on top would be much easier.

The researchers plan to develop a more realistic shop to test the technology more thoroughly, before hopefully beginning to roll it out in a live retail environment. It will be fascinating to track and see just how successful they prove to be.

27 July 2017

⇨ The above information is reprinted with kind permission from The Huffington Post UK. Please visit www.huffingtonpost.com for further information.

How do disabled people become disadvantaged by the way things are 'normally' done, and what will help things to change?

What is the problem?

Disabled people, with different impairments, are often disadvantaged or excluded, because of the way things are done. People trying to change things can feel powerless and trapped within existing systems, cultures and ways of doing things. The child protection system was recently described by one disabled parent as a "conveyor belt" that just moved them along without accounting for their support needs. There are frequently examples in the media about how disabled people are disadvantaged within the workplace or in their own communities. Health services are meant to be universal and equitable. However, because of the way things are routinely done, a person with learning disabilities or mental health problems might not be given time,

communication support or even life-saving treatment. People with dementia who have to go into hospital with an acute illness may be prevented from eating, because there is no one to support them with their food. Students and staff with physical disabilities who use wheelchairs may be excluded from classrooms and offices which are inaccessible, and above all this, services for disabled people are often designed and commissioned on their behalf, rather than by those who will use them.

What are the policies?

Policy and law tend to operate on the optimistic basis that guidance or legal statute will change people's behaviour. That is sometimes true to some extent. For instance, the 1989 Children Act states that every effort should be made to keep children with their

parents and this is backed by many other more recent legal and policy instruments, such as the 2014 Care Act and the statutory guidance *Working Together to Safeguard Children*, both of which promote early intervention and joint working. Yet services that can meet disabled parents' support needs are often lacking. At a wider universal level, the UN Convention on the Rights of Persons with Disabilities (UNCRPD) lays down principles about human rights, to which the UK is a signatory. Yet there are frequent examples of a gap between statements of Human Rights and the actual experiences of disabled people.

How can we look more closely at these issues?

The Dynamics of Social Practice Theory changes the focus of analysis – away from the micro level of behaviour change, and the macro ideas of governance and economics. Shove and her colleagues think about how social practices might be constituted and how they can change over time. As noted above, they see social practices as made up of three types of elements: meanings, materials and competences. Elements can shift and change over time, and that changes the way the actual practice is constituted. This is a different approach from other theories of change (which tend to either have a 'micro' focus on behaviour change, or a 'macro' focus on larger organisational forces of change). Social practices may fail to include disabled people, because of the meanings attached to 'disability'; for instance, hospitals may not have accessible training venues, as they fail to appreciate that staff could

be disabled. Social practices tend to recruit from particular populations (i.e. it is only some people who take up particular practices), and this can help us to see exactly how disabled people are excluded or how they 'misfit' into existing social practices. In turn, this can help us to analyse how these practices could be re-shaped by changing elements, so that they can recruit from a broader range of people, including those who are disabled.

What do we plan to do?

In our research we plan to analyse social practices as they occur in the everyday lives of disabled people, when they interact with those who are there to support them. Even with a supposedly 'empowering' personal budget, much depends on the ebb-and-flow of human interaction with frontline support staff. One of the strands in our research will be about making reasonable adjustments in hospitals. We are interested in how hospital doctors and other professionals assess patients and how they make adjustments to their practices to meet the needs of different disabled patients. Another focuses on the context of Higher Education where teaching and learning practices often unwittingly exclude disabled students and staff. We also plan to analyse social practices as they occur for parents with learning disabilities who are involved with social services due to concerns regarding the neglect of their children. We are interested in how social workers and other professionals assess and work with parents and how they can make adjustments to their practices to meet parents' support needs. All of these things can be seen as social practices.

How will this research help to get things changed?

We can change social practices best if we consider the whole jigsaw of interlinked elements involved. For instance, a patient with learning

disabilities who has acute breathing problems goes into hospital, and the consultant feels that he should not receive antibiotics, since he has had several similar attacks. Embedded in this medical decision is the attitude that the person's life might not be worth living, and so there are big challenges facing all of us in society, to change the meanings associated with the essential humanity and rights of people with learning disabilities. However, we would also need to consider the skills and competences that the consultant and medical team have, in communicating with this particular patient, who might need easy language and explanations of what is going on. The actual resources in the hospital, including for instance a hospital liaison nurse, and peer support, might have an effect on the practices which could save this patient's life. Social practice theory can help us to analyse in the round, and not just focus on one aspect of a problem.

Another example relates to disability in universities and workplaces like the NHS; if university and NHS hierarchies saw disabled staff as valuable assets, that would bring in its wake an attitude shift away from seeing people as 'burdens' on the system. Living with a long-term condition and managing crises could inspire how the NHS looks at service planning and frontline delivery, looking to patients as peers. Coming to academic knowledge from a different perspective of lived experience as a disabled person may be accredited and inform new academic subjects and how these subjects are taught. We are interested in the fundamental changes in attitude that might shift how things get done in universities and the NHS, and how disabled staff could lead changes in the technology of access, so that they have the same facilities as non-disabled staff.

Working to make links

Analysing social practices will help us to understand how practices are shaped and how they can change. However, there has seldom been any focus on social practices which 'exclude' people, and we aim to contribute to a wider understanding of the recruitment to particular social practices, and how they can be re-shaped to include disabled people. We suspect that much of this is about power inequalities, and that some social practices could be said to belong to the powerful majority, rather than to the oppressed minorities. We also want to link social practice theory with the types of analysis we are carrying out about social actions in conversation and discourse. We want to ensure that we work with ideas that are practical and will make a difference.

Key questions

⇨ Can social practice theory help us to understand the way disabled people experience barriers in different areas of life?

⇨ By disabled people taking action, and 'co-producing' change, can they shift and change the way social practices are shaped?

⇨ Is social practice theory enough, or can we make links with ideas about exclusion and inclusion, and power or inequality?

⇨ What will it take to move from theory to implementing practical change, so that we can apply it to make sure that policies do make a difference?

⇨ The above information is reprinted with kind permission from the University of Bristol. Please visit www.research-information, bristol.ac.uk for further information.

Families win Supreme Court appeals over 'unfair' bedroom tax

Panel upholds claim of Jacqueline Carmichael, who is disabled, and carers Paul and Susan Rutherford against housing law.

Owen Bowcott and Patrick Butler

Two families who claimed that the bedroom tax, which restricts housing subsidies, was unfair have won their appeals against the UK Government at the Supreme Court.

But five other claimants had their challenges dismissed at the country's highest court in a judgement that considered the specific circumstances of each individual applicant.

The seven-justice panel upheld the claims of Jacqueline Carmichael, who is disabled and cannot share a room with her husband, Jayson, as well as that of Paul and Susan Rutherford, who care for their severely disabled grandson, Warren, 17, in a specially adapted three-bedroom bungalow in Pembrokeshire, south Wales. Both had claimed discrimination under the European Convention on Human Rights.

Roger Toulson, who read out the main judgement, said: "Mrs Carmichael [who has spina bifida] cannot share a bedroom with her husband because of her disabilities... The Rutherfords need a regular overnight carer for their grandson, who has severe disabilities." Subjecting them to the bedroom tax was therefore "manifestly without reason".

The ruling pointed out that housing benefit regulations allow claimants to have an additional bedroom where children cannot share a bedroom because of a disability and that this exemption should be extended – as in the case of the Carmichaels – to adults.

The judgement follows a three-day hearing, which began on 29 February, at which lawyers representing adults with disabilities and adult carers went

to the Supreme Court to argue two sets of cases.

The claimants, who were represented by Central England Law Centre, Leigh Day and the Child Poverty Action Group, said disabled people were being discriminated against because they were subject to regulations made for the able-bodied.

Since April 2013, housing benefit for people in the social rented sector deemed to have a spare bedroom has been reduced by 14% and people deemed to have two or more spare bedrooms have had their housing benefit reduced by 25%. In these claims the issue was over whether disability meant they could move to smaller accommodation.

Cases brought by the other families were dismissed even though the court said it had "profound sympathy" for some of the claimants who lost. There were cries of "shame" from some of them when the judgement was announced.

Paul and Susan Rutherford were in court to hear the result. "It's been a three-and-a-half-year battle," Paul said afterwards. "We have had to keep re-applying for benefit all the time. It hasn't been easy. I'm relieved, happy that a lot of other people who are in the same position as us will benefit from this decision.

"Warren cannot communicate but knows that we have gone up to London. If we had lost we would have had to downsize and fit out a new property with ceiling hoists and special adaptations. If we moved to a two-bedroom place we wouldn't have had anywhere to employ carers. Health and safety would not have allowed it.

"Our [present] bungalow was fitted out for Warren and the spare room was intended to be used by a carer so that he or she could stay overnight."

Sophie Earnshaw of the Child Poverty Action Group, who represented the Rutherfords, said: "This is a great result. Today marks the end of a three-year ordeal for the family. This means that those with disabled children who need overnight care will not be subject to the bedroom tax. Thousands of people will no longer be affected by the bedroom tax.

"For Paul and Sue this means they will be able to move on with their lives and be able to care for Warren at home. We hope the Government will repeal the bedroom tax in its entirety."

Rosa Curling, a solicitor at the law firm Leigh Day, who represented the Carmichaels, said: "This is an extremely important and welcome decision which recognises that the Government cannot trample over people's rights in the name of austerity.

"Our clients had a very clear medical need for two bedrooms and it's disappointing that the Government chose to fight this case for three years, putting our clients through a long period of uncertainty. Our clients are delighted that justice has been done and they can now start to move on with their lives knowing that their rights as a disabled person and their right to a family life together will be respected."

But the claim brought by a woman identified only as A, who is a victim of domestic violence, was dismissed by a majority of five to two justices on the Supreme Court.

Her predicament has been highlighted by campaigners concerned that women who have had their homes specially adapted because of security threats from ex-partners will be forced to move to smaller and potentially less secure homes at great cost.

Rebekah Carrier, a solicitor with the law firm Hopkin Murray Beskine, who represented A, said she would appeal to the European Court of Human Rights. "My client has been subjected to the bedroom tax because she was allocated a three-bedroom house 25 years ago, through no choice of her own, due to a shortage of two-bedroom houses," Carrier said.

"She is a vulnerable single parent who has been a victim of rape and assault. Her life remains at risk and she is terrified. As a result, she has

been given the protection of a multi-agency network and had her home specially adapted by the police, at great expense."

Brenda Hale, who was in the minority, observed in her dissenting judgement: "The state has provided Ms A with such a safe haven. It allocated her a three-bedroomed house when she did not need one. That was not her choice. It later fortified that house and put in place a detailed plan to keep her and her son safe.

"Reducing her housing benefit by reference to the number of bedrooms puts at risk her ability to stay there. Because of its special character, it will be difficult if not impossible for her to move elsewhere and that would certainly put the state to yet further expense."

A spokesperson for the Department for Work and Pensions said: "It is welcome that the court found in our favour in five out of the seven cases. The court also agreed with our view that discretionary housing payments are generally an appropriate and lawful way to provide assistance to those who need extra help.

"In the two specific cases where the court did not find in our favour, we will take steps to ensure we comply with the judgement in due course. In most cases, local authorities are best placed to understand the needs of their residents, which is why we will have given them over £1 billion by the end of this parliament for discretionary housing payments to ensure that people in difficult situations don't lose out."

Among campaigners in court to hear the judgement was Paula Peters, of Disabled People Against Cuts. She said: "While we are pleased for Jayson and Paul, who had their claims upheld, we are very concerned for disabled people who are in adapted property and who need a spare bedroom. The court ruled that the decision does not cover them in specially adapted property and they would have to

move to another adapted property of a smaller size, of which there is a great shortage."

The Rev. Paul Nicholson, of Taxpayers Against Poverty, said: "I have watched people lose weight because they can't survive on cuts imposed by the bedroom tax. It's a bad law."

Claire Glasman, of the anti-poverty group WinVisible, said: "The bedroom tax is an attack on low-income people. It only affects people in social housing. Councils have been discriminatory in how they administer housing payments.

"We are worried that women and children are going to die as a result of the ruling on women fleeing domestic violence. There's no safety for them in this judgement. [The judges] are picking and choosing in disability cases. Why should people have to lose their homes?"

Debbie Abrahams MP, the shadow work and pensions secretary, said: "The bedroom tax is a cruel and unnecessary policy. It is widely despised by the British public, who see it what for what it is; a callous attempt to punish low-income, social housing tenants. A Labour government will scrap [it], ending the misery faced by thousands across the country."

9 November 2016

⇨ The above information is reprinted with kind permission from *The Guardian*. Please visit www.theguardian.com for further information.

End exam discrimination for doctors with disabilities

The BMA should work with medical royal colleges and the GMC to end exam discrimination towards doctors with disabilities, a conference has heard.

Members attending the annual BMA junior doctors conference on 13 May backed calls for the association to consult with colleges and the medical regulator in reviewing the reasonable adjustment process for postgraduate exams.

Manchester foundation doctor 3 psychiatrist Gursharan Johal said that too many doctors with additional needs were being unfairly penalised by a "one-size-fits-all" approach to examination adjustments.

She said: "There are more trainees with additional needs working and training in the NHS than ever before.

"These may be physical needs, or they may be educational difficulties which can affect reading, writing or speaking. Reasonable adjustments are not a one-size-fits-all concept like our esteemed [medical] colleges think."

Dr Johal, who is herself dyslexic, said junior doctors with disabilities often faced additional challenges and barriers during the exam process, with the system too standardised to cater for individual needs.

She called for all medical royal colleges to adopt reasonable adjustments, adding that a doctor's chosen speciality should not dictate the level of support they received in examinations and assessment.

"We have a situation now where trainees request adjustments when they apply to take their exams and are often only told what their adjustments are days before the examinations, with no choice for changing these," she said

"This is clear disability discrimination to our junior doctors taking their exams to work in our health service to care for our patients. These people need a fair run at their postgraduate exams."

"Under the 2010 Equality Act, universities are required to make reasonable adjustments prior to a student commencing study, including areas such as mobility support, changes to work or on-call rotas and extensions on deadlines"

Medical schools should have a disability support adviser to guide students and help provide assessment as to what support might be needed during foundation years and beyond.

BMA representative body chair Anthea Mowat endorsed the plan but highlighted that the GMC had recently launched a working group into the ways in which access to medicine could be improved for those with disabilities.

18 May 2017

⇨ The above information is reprinted with kind permission from the British Medical Association. Please visit www.bma.org.uk for further information.

Young carers at risk of not fulfilling their ambitions, show new figures on Young Carers Awareness Day

"When I grow up" – being a young carer should not mean that a child's future hopes, dreams and ambitions are shattered.

A new survey by Carers Trust has revealed that young carers across the UK are struggling to get the most out of their education and are in danger of not fulfilling their ambitions due to their caring role.

Of the young adult carers we surveyed over half (53%) were having problems in coping with schoolwork with nearly 60% struggling to meet deadlines. A startling number – 73% – told us that they have to take time out of school or learning specifically to care for a family member. A third admitted that they have to skip school most weeks.

"I wanted to be like everyone else…"

With 82% of young adult carers also reporting stress, a worrying picture is emerging, revealing the extent to which their caring role is severely affecting their future choices.

A female young adult carer says:

"I wanted to be like everyone else and go to university, but I suffered a breakdown, and only achieved the lowest grade in my degree. I couldn't go far from my parents as I had responsibilities and their lives really went to s**t with me not being there to run the house. I haven't gone back to live there as it is no good for my mental health but their struggle is far greater now which brings me a lot of guilt."

700,000 young carers in the UK

There are an estimated 700,000 children and young people across the UK, some as young as five-years-old, who are caring for family members. This is likely a conservative figure as many are hidden from view.

Most care for a parent or other close family member, day in, day out, and shockingly, at least 13,000 young carers are providing care for over 50 hours a week on top of their studies.

A young carer explains how caring has made it more of a challenge to achieve his dream job:

"Because I became a carer during my GCSEs which resulted in me having anxiety and depression, so my focus in school and in lessons went down. And most of the time due to my self-harm and anxiety problems I wouldn't go to my lessons."

Giving young carers support to achieve their dreams and ambitions

Gail Scott-Spicer, Chief Executive of Carers Trust, said:

"Our new survey data paints a very worrying picture for the hundreds of thousands of young carers across the UK, if the right support and guidance isn't in place. Being a young carer should not mean that a child's future hopes, dreams, and ambitions are shattered.

"We know young carers miss or cut short on average 10 weeks of school a year as a direct result of their caring role, and those aged between 16 and 18 years are twice as likely to be not in education, employment or training (NEET). We must make sure young

carers get the support they need so they can enjoy their childhoods like any other young person and achieve their ambitions.

"On Young Carers Awareness Day, Carers Trust wants to reach hidden young carers up and down the UK, who desperately need our help."

Getting involved in Young Carers Awareness Day

Young Carers Awareness Day aims to raise awareness of the plight of young carers and we are asking people to spot the signs of caring, such as being late or absent from school or behavioural issues. Swift identification of young carers will ensure they get vital support.

26 January 2017

⇨ The above information is reprinted with kind permission from Carerstrust. Please visit www. carers.org for further information.

© 2018 Carerstrust

No future: young carers are sacrificing ambitions to look after loved ones

Children looking after a family member are making decisions about their future in the context of their role, often limiting their options and stunting their ambitions.

An article from **The Conversation.**

THE CONVERSATION

By Oonagh Robison, Public Health Research Specialist, Glasgow Centre for Population Health, Univesity of Glasgow

There are around 700,000 young carers across the UK looking after a parent or a family member. In Glasgow, these young people make up around 12 per cent of children aged 11–18, and now a new study has found that their duties and responsibilities are preventing around half of them from going on to university or college after school.

According to a 2014 NHS survey of 11,000 pupils across the city, one in eight secondary school-age pupils in Glasgow is providing care for someone at home. Not only do these pupils care for someone with a disability, long-term illness, mental health or substance issue, they also have poorer outcomes for their own health and future expectations.

Our new study for the Glasgow Centre for Population Health (GCPH) found that when asked what they thought they would do once they had left school, young carers were almost 50 per cent less likely to say that they thought they would go on to university or college when compared with pupils who had no caring duties.

The type of care given by young carers can vary considerably, from doing household chores to physical assistance, such as moving or lifting, to more intimate care, such as washing, dressing and help with going to the toilet, and providing emotional support.

Low expectations

That carers – and young carers generally – are more likely to be found in deprived areas and in low-income families shows how caring has become associated with, and compounded by, other forms of disadvantage. Data from the 2011 Census shows the prevalence of caring in Scotland to be higher in West Central Scotland, the area with the largest concentration of deprivation. Glasgow also has higher than average levels of long-term sick or disabled adults, problem drug use, and alcohol-related deaths.

Previous research has found that young people in lone-parent families are also more likely to become young carers, and with 40 per cent of households with dependent children in Glasgow headed by a single parent, it is perhaps unsurprising that the numbers are so high.

As well as facing economic disadvantage, our study also found that carers had poorer physical and mental health. The association with mental health and emotional and behavioural difficulties was especially strong for the quarter of young carers looking after someone with a mental health problem, and the ten per cent caring for someone with a drug or alcohol problem.

The hidden carers

The attainment gap between richer and poorer students has long been recognised, and strategies such as the Scottish Attainment Challenge from the Scottish Government aim to make a difference by channelling more money into schools.

But low attainment isn't just about poverty – it's also about young people not having the confidence, opportunities or the freedom to choose and shape their future. Young carers can be bound geographically, physically and in terms of their time, all of which have an impact on what they think they can do when they leave school.

Previous research has found that not only do young carers tend to have poorer educational achievements, but employment and education decisions are made within the context and constraints of their caring role, often limiting their options and stunting their ambitions.

These young carers are not just experiencing multiple disadvantages, a third of them are also, our study found, struggling along without anyone outside the family knowing about their caring role. This may go some way to explaining the higher prevalence found in our study – 12 per cent – which was higher than previous estimates.

The discrepancy between the high prevalence found in our report and the lower official figures could be down to many reasons. Some of those defined as young carers don't actually realise that they are providing care, and many do not know that there is support available. Others may choose to conceal their carer status due to fears around the stigma of caring, and others may be afraid of outside intervention if anyone discovers their role at home.

The type of care that they are providing can also have an impact on the number of hidden carers. Those with family members with more stigmatised conditions such as mental health or substance issues may fear the consequences if their status is revealed.

Rights of the child?

The United Nations Convention on the Rights of the Child (UNCRC) outlines some general rights for children, such as every child has the right to a happy life and to develop to the maximum extent possible, as well as recognising that they need guidance and space to be young people and to learn, play and enjoy positive futures. Our findings suggest that being a young carer can impact negatively on these rights.

The introduction of the Carers (Scotland) Act (2016) means that by April 2018, local authorities and health boards will have a duty to provide Young Carer 'statements', which will identify support needs and personal goals and development. This will be an important opportunity to ensure that all young carers are supported enough to have the chance to realise their full potential.

24 September 2017

⇨ The above information is reprinted with kind permission from *The Conversation*. Please visit www.theconversation for further information.

Being a young carer – your rights

A young carer is someone aged 18 or under who helps look after a relative who has a condition, such as a disability, illness, mental health condition, or a drug or alcohol problem.

Most young carers look after one of their parents or care for a brother or sister. They do extra jobs in and around the home, such as cooking, cleaning, or helping someone to get dressed and move around.

Some children give a lot of physical help to a brother or sister who is disabled or ill. Along with doing things to help your brother or sister, you may also be giving emotional support to both your sibling and your parents.

Your choices about caring

Some people start caring at a very young age and don't really realise they are carers. Other young people become carers overnight. If someone in your family needs to be looked after, you may really want to help them.

But young carers shouldn't do the same things as adult carers, nor should they be spending a lot of their time caring for someone, as this can get in the way of them doing well at school and doing the same kinds of things as other children or young people.

It's important you decide how much and what type of care you're willing or able to give, or whether you should be a carer at all.

You need to decide whether you're the right person to offer the care that the person you look after needs. All disabled adults are entitled to support from their local authority, depending on their needs, so they should not have to rely on their children to care for them. It's important for social services to ensure the whole family feels supported and comfortable with your role.

Young carers' rights

The law is changing for young carers, and from April 2015 a social worker from your local authority must visit to carry out a young carers needs assessment to decide what kind of help you and your family might need if you or your parents request this.

If the local authority has already carried out one of these assessments before, they must carry out another one if you or your parents feel that your needs or circumstances have changed.

A young carer's needs assessment must decide whether it is appropriate for you to care for someone else – and this includes taking into account whether you want to be a carer. The local authority must also look at your education, training, leisure opportunities and your views about your future. When assessing a young carer they must always ask about your wishes and involve you, your parents and anyone else you or your parents want to be involved.

All these people should receive a written record of the assessment. This should include whether the local authority thinks you need support, whether their services could provide you with that support, and whether they will give you that support. It should also explain what you can do if you or your parents disagree with the assessment.

Provided that you both agree, the local authority can assess both your needs as a young carer and the needs of the person you care for, at the same time.

If you're 16 or over, and you're not in full-time education you may be eligible for help finding work as well as help with your family's finances, for instance through benefits such as Carer's Allowance. Your assessment is the best place to find out about what is available in your situation.

15 January 2015

⇨ The above information is reprinted with kind permission from NHS Choices. Please visit www.nhs.uk for further information.

Hard evidence: is the number of disabled people in work on the up?

***An article from* The Conversation.**

THE CONVERSATION

Victoria Wass, Reader in Economics, Cardiff University

If you keep track of key measures of disability equality in the UK, you'll know that the gap in employment rates between disabled and non-disabled working-age people has gone down over the past 15 years.

Many experts have flagged this trend: Dame Carol Black in her influential 2008 review of health and work, DWP indicators 2009-2015 and a recent editorial in the *British Medical Journal*. It is on the basis of this trend that the UK appears to be more successful than its neighbours in OECD comparisons in integrating disabled people into the workplace.

But another look at the evidence puts this into question.

Amidst these reports that find a decrease in the disability employment gap, another group of researchers – including authors of two papers in the *BMJ* and a report by leading expert Richard Berthoud – have written about how it is going up. Partly this is explained by a difference in time period (starting from 1998 compared to the late 1970s). But, even focusing on the same period (1998–2012), this latter group find no change in the disability employment gap.

Without explanation or reconciliation (or even a dialogue between the two groups), the most basic question in disability-employment research: "has the disability employment gap gone down?" cannot be answered. This was the subject of recent research I conducted with my colleagues Ben Baumberg and Melanie Jones. Resolving the issue is crucially important if we are to judge the effects of equality legislation and the Government's Work Programme, which seeks to get the long-term unemployed back into work. And also to judge the 2015 Conservative Party Manifesto commitment "to halve the disability employment gap".

Different surveys

The difference in trends arises from choice of survey. Those who find that disabled people are catching up in terms of their employment rate have used the Labour Force Survey, while those who find no change have used the General Household Survey. Importantly both surveys are collected and published by the UK Government, are based on a random sample of households and measure disability in the same way, namely as a longstanding illness or disability that limits daily activities.

There are lots of differences between surveys which could give rise to differences in disability employment gaps – though not perhaps differences in trends in those gaps. These include differences in the methods used to interview people (such as telephone or face-to-face), differences in question wording and differences in areas of the country included.

Looking into all of these details and harmonising the data by restricting our analysis to only those parts of the surveys that are strictly comparable, we compared standardised employment gaps across the different surveys.

We also included results from a third high-quality survey that no-one had previously used in this context, the Health Survey for England.

The trends for all three surveys show that the same puzzling differences in trends remain after harmonisation. The Labour Force Survey (LFS) shows an improving trend towards greater equality in employment. But this trend is not evident in the Health Survey for England (HSE) or the General Household Survey (GHS).

Explaining the difference

One potentially important difference in the LFS is that the proportion of working-age people reporting disability has been rising steadily and there is a strong association between the level of disability reporting and the disability employment rate in the LFS. This makes sense – the people who move across the borderline between reporting and not reporting a disability are likely to be less severely disabled than people who will definitely report a disability.

In contrast, in the HSE and GHS, disability reporting has been relatively stable – if anything it's been falling over time – and it is not strongly linked to the employment rate. Until we understand why disability has increased in the LFS (but not in the other surveys), we cannot conclude that employment prospects for disabled people have improved.

In the meantime, however, the LFS measure is the main policy-evaluation tool used by the Government in formulating its policies towards the employment of disabled people. This is unsatisfactory. Since the LFS trend is inconsistent with trends in the others, it should not be relied upon as the sole indicator of the disability employment gap in the UK. Until we can explain this contradictory evidence, governments should stop claiming success in the integration of disabled people into the workplace.

8 October 2015

⇨ The above information is reprinted with kind permission from *The Conversation*. Please visit www.theconversation for further information.

One million disabled people blocked from work, finds CSJ

According to a new report by the Centre for Social Justice (CSJ), one million disabled people who are currently out of work want to find employment, but are blocked from doing so.

Under 48 per cent of people with disabilities are employed, compared to 80 per cent of non-disabled people.

Out-of-work benefits for disabled people cost £19 billion a year, while the Exchequer loses £21 billion–£29 billion a year in foregone tax and national insurance revenue due to health-related joblessness.

Chief Executive of the CSJ, Andy Cook, commented:

"The disability employment gap is a social justice issue. Despite having one of the most robust and flexible labour markets in the world, millions of disabled people in the UK are not able to enjoy the financial, health and emotional gains associated with employment.

"By letting this happen, we are undermining our economy and we are shredding the social fabric of our society.

"It is time to change this. Employers have everything to gain from increasing the number of disabled people in their workforce. The reality is that employers who do not hire disabled people miss out on talented, committed employees.

"This report provides ways of meeting the challenges that disabled people face in the labour market, offering a clear blueprint for a more inclusive, productive and robust labour force – one in which everybody, no matter what challenges they face, can achieve their full potential."

According to a CSJ poll, almost two-thirds (63 per cent) of HR decision makers think there are barriers to hiring disabled people. Their biggest two concerns are ability to do the job (34 per cent) and the cost of making reasonable adjustments in the workplace (31 per cent).

Only a third (33 per cent) of employers have hired a disabled person in the last year, and fewer than one in ten (nine per cent) of employers think there is usually a strong business case for hiring a disabled person.

The report also finds that the Government has failed to make businesses aware of the advice and services it offers to help employ disabled people.

While 300,000 people a year fall out of work due to health conditions, the 'Fit for Work' programme, which offers employees and employers free work-related health advice to help reduce sickness absence, had an uptake of only around 9,000 people in 18 months.

Just 25 per cent of employers know what Fit for Work is and understand the help that they can get from this service.

The Government will not succeed in its pledge to halve the disability employment gap if it does not help employers overcome their misgivings about hiring disabled people.

The CSJ is recommending that Fit for Work should be rebranded. The report states:

"At its heart, it is a national occupational health service – free at the point of delivery.

"It should be named to reflect just that."

The think tank is also calling for the Government to introduce a duty for employers who do not have private occupational health services to have an early conversation with Fit for Work where employees have been absent for three weeks, to help prevent absences becoming long-term.

Halving the disability employment gap was a Conservative Party manifesto commitment. In the 2015 Autumn Statement, the Government reaffirmed its intention to narrow the disability employment gap. A full report of proposals is expected in the coming months.

Kirsty McHugh, Chief Executive of Employment Related Services Association, who contributed to the report, commented:

"Today's report is a timely and important reminder that we must do more to help disabled people to enter the labour market. It is a moral outrage that millions of disabled people who can and want to work are currently unable to do so. It also makes no business sense.

"Bold action is required if the Government is serious about halving the disability employment gap. In this light, the report sets out practical but significant steps to meet this challenge, including harnessing the apprenticeship levy funding and investing in specialist employment support.

"To reach its target, the government must invest in supporting disabled people; not only because the Chancellor will reap the financial benefits, but also for the health and emotional gains for each individual. Ultimately, it is simply the right thing to do."

CEO of Business Disability Forum, Diane Lightfoot, who was also on the report's working group commented:

"Business Disability Forum welcomes this report and in particular, the recognition that engaging employers

is fundamental to closing the disability employment gap.

"Many of our members and partners are truly leading the way when it comes to recruitment and retention of disabled employees.

"However, almost two-thirds of employers surveyed for this report perceive barriers to employing someone with a disability with one of the largest concerns being around work place adjustments. Yet, not only are most adjustments tiny, but Access to Work can meet the costs of those that would be unreasonable for an employer to pay.

"Far more needs to be done if this remarkably effective benefit is to move from being the Government's 'best kept secret' to become a significant enabler towards work."

Tim Cooper, Chief Executive of United Response, disability charity and supported employment specialist on the report's working group commented:

"We welcome the publication of this report today. For the last two decades statistics around disability

employment have hardly changed and remain shockingly low.

"People with learning disabilities are the most marginalised of all disability groups when it comes to employment, with only 5.8 per cent currently in paid employment.

"Although 65 per cent of people with learning disability want to work this group's employment rate continues to fall at a time when all others rise.

"Through our own work we know that access to specialist employment support opens the job market to people with learning disabilities. We are pleased to see recommendations in the report today supporting this point by calling for specific specialist employment support contracts to be made available for people with learning disabilities."

27 March 2017

⇨ The above information is reprinted with kind permission from The Centre for Social Justice. Please visit www.centreforsocialjustice.org.uk for further information.

© 2018 The Centre for Social Justice

An inclusive future – barriers to work

An extract from an article by the Fabian Society.

By Mark Atkinson

Many disabled people face barriers getting in to, progressing in and staying in work. Removing these barriers requires a cross-government approach, writes Mark Atkinson.

For many disabled people, working is key to living independently.

Having a steady income is all the more important if you are disabled, given the extra costs of around £550 every month that come with managing a condition or impairment. But work is about much more than wages. Carving out a career and building skills, expertise and relationships along the way is often a hugely fulfilling experience.

Yet less than half of all disabled people are currently in work – 48 per cent of disabled people are in work compared to 80 per cent of non-disabled people. Whilst it's true, that more disabled people are in work now, than ever before, the substantial difference, between the two rates – the disability employment gap – has barely shifted over the last ten years.

Today, disabled people still face a number of barriers getting in to work, staying at work and progressing in their careers.

At Scope, we campaign for the world to become a place where disabled people have the same opportunities as everybody else.

Tackling barriers within employment is central to this. We're pleased to have worked with the Fabian Society on this series of essays, bringing together the experiences and expertise of disabled people, leaders in employment research, as well as key figures within the Labour Party committed to ensuring the future world of work is as inclusive as it can be.

The Conservative Government has made a welcome commitment to halve the disability employment gap by 2020, but the success of this hinges on cross-party collaboration. It is essential that the Labour Party takes on a dual role in ensuring this objective is reached. On the one hand, Labour should support the initiative, adopting it as a shared goal, while on the other, it must hold the Government to account, making sure measures introduced over the coming years will be sufficient to deliver the change disabled people want to see.

Beyond this, as Labour starts to explore the changing world of work, it is important that the experiences and aspirations of the almost 13 million disabled people living in the UK are listened to and taken into account when developing policy now and in the future. The new Changing Work Centre established by the Fabian Society and Community presents an exciting opportunity to develop a plan for a future world of work built with disabled people at the centre. This should help shape a vision where opportunities to find and progress in work are open to everyone.

Disabled people face a range of barriers at all stages of their careers. At the root of this is insufficient support for working disabled people and outdated workplace culture. 85 per cent of disabled people feel employer attitudes haven't changed since 2012.

Tackling these barriers is no simple feat, but will be essential to making the future world of work inclusive of disabled people.

This calls for creative and lasting solutions to bridge the gap between policy and practice when it comes to recruiting, supporting and developing disabled people.

Getting in to work

Until now, mainstream support in to work has not been successful with disabled people.

Schemes like the Work Programme, which take a one-size-fits-all approach, just don't deliver. Requiring people to take part in a programme or risk losing their out-of-work benefits has led to poor results for disabled people, with the programme seeing a success rate of seven per cent.

By contrast, the specialist Work Choice scheme has had a much higher success rate, with 59 per cent of disabled people who started the programme in 2014/15 in work by June 2016. There are two key reasons for this – participation in Work Choice is voluntary, not mandated, and the programme is designed to offer specialist support disabled people might need to find and stay in work.

Disabled people should be able to get advice and support around employment both in and out of work. This should come from specialist organisations with staff who have an understanding of the full range of barriers disabled people face when looking for work. They should be able to choose if and when they participate in an employment support programme, without facing any risk to their financial support.

As Felix Labwo and Lauren Pitt illustrate in their contributions to this publication, many disabled people who disclose a condition or impairment in a job application simply aren't considered for roles.

In fact, 74 per cent of disabled people we surveyed felt they had lost out on a job opportunity because of their impairment.

This just isn't fair. All too often, employers perceive disabled people as risky hires.

All employers, from banks to hospitals, large firms to political parties, should recognise the huge potential that comes with opening up a workforce to the widest pool of talent available.

Progressing in their careers

Disabled people face barriers once they're in work too, often missing out on opportunities to develop new skills and move up in their careers. The two most common forms of workplace discrimination disabled people face are being given fewer responsibilities and not being promoted. When these opportunities are afforded to their non-disabled colleagues, a progression gap starts to emerge.

Staying in work

Getting the right support and resources is essential for many disabled people to do their jobs. But too often, disabled people leave the workplace altogether following a change in their health when the right adjustments or support could have supported them to stay in their role.

Making adjustments

We know that increasing numbers of people are falling out of work due to illness or disability. While in some cases that may be the right route to take, it is vital that disabled people are given an opportunity to explore how they might best be supported to carry on working if their circumstances change. Only 42 per cent of people who receive the out of work benefit Employment and Support Allowance were offered an adjustment before they left their job in 2014.

Most employers do understand their legal obligation to offer workplace adjustments to disabled people – 96 per cent of employers have a workplace adjustment procedure in place. Yet, policy doesn't always translate into practice. Many employers continue to struggle to understand their role in supporting disabled employees.

To drive real change, we believe employers need industry-specific guidance on workplace adjustments. This should be targeted towards whole organisations, with line managers getting the training and resources they need to best support disabled members of their teams and enable them to perform to their full potential.

We know that many disabled people chose to work part-time to manage their health and wellbeing, with 13 per cent reporting that their decision to work reduced hours related to their impairment or condition.

A further 26 per cent of disabled people in work would prefer to work shorter hours if they could. Scope's own research supports this, with 48 per cent of disabled employees telling us modified hours were key to staying in work.

This was certainly true for Gill, who found out she needed dialysis just a month after starting her new job:

"I thought, 'it's all going to go wrong again now. I'm going to have to stop working.' I told my boss, and she was absolutely fine with it. She said, 'If you can do afternoon dialysis and come to work in the morning, that's fine'. Now, not every company would let me do that."

While all employees have a right to request flexible working, arrangements like Gill's between a disabled person and their employer are still startlingly rare.

Flexible working should be at the heart of ambitions to create inclusive workplaces. All types of flexible working, including flexitime, remote working and flexible approaches to sickness absence, should be built in to this drive to make the UK's workplaces fit for the future.

Driving a cross-government approach

Changes to workplace culture and practices alone will not be sufficient to drive the societal change needed to make sure disabled people have the same opportunities at work as everyone else. Disabled people face a number of other barriers that can make working more difficult.

One of these is not getting the right social care. Many disabled people get support to live independently through a social care package. Scope research has found 79 per cent of disabled people who use social care feel it is important in enabling them to work or look for work. Among younger disabled people (aged 17–30) using social care, only 15 per cent were getting support with working, and only 13 per cent were getting support with looking for work.

Social care should be better aligned to disabled people's needs and aspirations around living independently. This should factor in support they may need around looking for or staying at work.

Another barrier to work is getting the right financial support. Disabled people face extra costs amounting to an average of £550 per month as a result of

their condition or impairment. Personal Independence Payments (PIP) play a vital role in supporting disabled people to overcome financial barriers to work. In a recent survey of people who receive PIP and its predecessor DLA, more than half said that PIP or DLA was important in helping them to work. Among those looking for work, 37 per cent said that these payments were important in helping them to do so.

For PIP to play a meaningful role in supporting disabled people to meet the extra costs they face both while looking for work and at work, it has to be protected from means-testing. And to secure this support within the future world of work, the level of PIP should grow in line with inflation.

Only through a truly cross-government approach can these wider barriers to work be overcome. Policy makers should consider each of the solutions set out here as single components within a wider whole. Whoever is able to take this whole-system approach to disability employment will be in the best position to drive meaningful and lasting change in the British workplace.

Labour has set itself a bold ambition of understanding and planning for a future world of work. It is positive to see the party exploring what changes might affect the UK labour market and considering what innovative practices could be developed in response. For this project to have maximum impact, people who face barriers to participating in some or all of the labour market as it is must be at the centre of plans for change.

To drive real change in working opportunities for disabled people, Labour should look to re-think how employers are supported to set up and run their workplaces.

September 2016

⇨ The above extract is reprinted with kind permission from the Fabian Society. Please visit www.fabians.org.uk for further information.

Employers may discriminate against autism without realising

Employers often think they're communicating well, but they use 'neurotypical' standards of interacting, writes Brett Heasman, PhD student, Department of Psychological and Behavioural Science at the London School of Economics.

Autism is a lifelong developmental disability that affects how people connect and relate to others and also how they experience the world around them.

Most non-autistic people are not aware of the complex ways in which autistic people experience the world and are not adequately prepared for interacting or working with autistic people. Autism is a 'hidden' disability, with no external physical signs, and it encompasses a huge range of people, behaviours, abilities and challenges which, for many non-autistic people, takes time to appreciate and understand.

The gap in public understanding of autism has very real consequences for employment prospects. Only 16 per cent of autistic adults are in full-time work despite 77 per cent of those unemployed wanting to work. This employment figure has not changed since 2007 and remains significantly lower than the average employment figures for people belonging to other disability categories (47%). In short, something is going seriously wrong in the workplace for autistic people to be so disproportionally unemployed.

Social world and impression management challenges

That autistic people are disadvantaged is not surprising, given how we have built a world heavily dependent on tight social coordination with others. Access to any employment opportunity requires candidates to navigate the social encounter of the interview, while even getting to the stage of an interview in the first place requires the ability to build social capital and network with others. For people who have life-long difficulties in social interaction, the social process of finding employment remains a considerable obstacle. A lack of eye contact, or a silence that lasts too long can have very negative consequences for rapport. Yet autistic people may give off these signals unintentionally, which is why employers need to look past small-scale social cues to take a broader perspective on what is meaningful interaction.

Relationship challenges and the 'double empathy problem'

Building professional relationships is another critical issue. I have worked throughout my doctorate with a charity that supports young autistic adults, and have seen how quickly professional and personal relationships can break down.

A recent study conducted by myself and Dr Alex Gillespie, LSE, has shed new light on why this may be the case. We examined family relationships between autistic adults and their family members and found that many misunderstandings did not always originate from the autistic adult. Family members were often incorrectly taking the perspective of autistic relations, seeing them as more 'egocentrically anchored' in their own perspective than they actually were. This misunderstanding raises an important question regarding the assumptions used by non-autistic people to evaluate autistic people. It is evidence of the 'double empathy problem', a persisting gap in mutual understanding because both sides of a given autistic/non-autistic relationship have different normative expectations and assumptions about what the 'other' thinks.

Case study of a professional autistic relationship

I recently visited a workplace where a trainee had been diagnosed with autism and was finding that his relationship with his employers was very difficult to manage. In particular, he had very low self-esteem, was uncomfortable with the constant change to his schedule, and did not like having to attend meetings particularly because it left him feeling criticised which would inevitably affect his other activities for the day.

From the employer's perspective, they were very keen to show that they had been adapting to his particular way of working within what they perceived to be reasonable adjustments. However, there were still some points that I had to clarify to the employers which highlight the 'double empathy problem' in action.

For example, it emerged that in meetings, the autistic employee would often misunderstand what had been said. In response, the employer stressed that they had no problem with the meeting being stopped if the autistic employee wanted to ask a question or clarify a point of discussion. Yet this is a problematic assumption, because the autistic employee may not realise a misunderstanding has taken place until much later, when it had manifested into a problem, and even if he did recognise in the moment that there was a misunderstanding, it should not be assumed that he would be able to speak up instantly.

Speaking up is a very difficult social skill, where one must assess the dialogue, look for moments of verbal interjection, and give a non-verbal signal to 'take control of the floor' just prior to speaking. It requires an acute reading of the social situation, and no small amount of confidence to perform.

Another challenge was the employer was very focused on developing strategies for the employee to embrace and work with 'constructive criticism' in order to improve the way in which the team worked as a whole. I suggested that it might also be a good idea to run over the positive things which the autistic employee had done. From the employer's perspective, this had not seemed particularly necessary because many of the positive aspects were deemed obvious. However, when I spoke to the autistic employee it was very clear that he had no idea what it was that he did well, and because of his low self-esteem, would often downplay compliments.

This highlights another disjuncture in the relationship that needed to be addressed. The employer needed to give much more positive feedback, even on tasks that seemed obvious and inconsequential, because it could not be assumed that the autistic employee shared the same level of certainty about what was good or bad practice.

These two examples show how the employer believed good communication was already in place, when in fact their model of communication was framed around 'neurotypical' standards of interacting. Undoubtedly the employer was keen to do the best for managing the professional relationship and had already made many adjustments, but these examples show how deep-rooted our social reading of others is ingrained, and how much opportunity remains to improve public and employer understanding of autism through listening to what autistic people have to say.

⇨ The above information is reprinted with kind permission from the London School of Economics and Political Science. Please visit www.Lse.ac.uk for further information.

Rethinking disability at work

Recommendations, polling data and key statistics. An extract from an article by The Centre for Social Justice.

In work

Some employers are leading the way in recognising the strengths disabled individuals bring to their workforces, building healthy working environments and managing illness well.

Others lag behind. The key challenge is to provide these employers with the knowledge and skills they need to become more confident about disability and to illuminate the business case for employing disabled individuals.

Just 47.9 per cent of disabled people are employed, compared to 80.1 per cent of non-disabled people – to halve the gap between these two figures, 1.2 million disabled people will need to find employment.

The UK's disability employment gap is higher than that found in 21 other European countries, and those in Luxembourg, Sweden, France and Turkey are less than ten per cent.

Making apprenticeships work for disabled people

Recommendation 1

By allowing people to grow their skills and knowledge, apprenticeships increase employability. The new apprenticeships levy will allow the Government to double investment in apprenticeships to £2.5 billion by 2020, relative to 2010 levels. This is an exciting opportunity to create new employment opportunities for disabled people who, on average, have fewer qualifications than non-disabled people.

Current funding plans provide financial support for employers and training providers who train 19–24-year-old care leavers, or those who have Education, Health and Care plans (EHC plans). But not all employers know what an EHC plan is and the process individual have to go through to obtain EHC plans is not always straightforward.

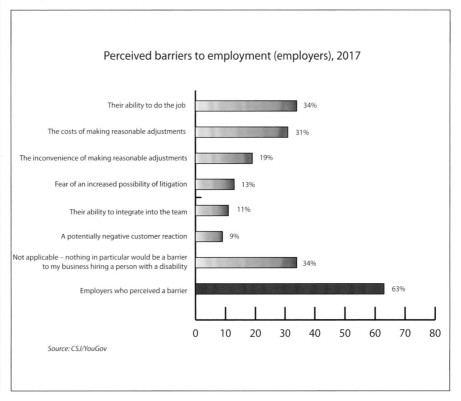

Perceived barriers to employment (employers), 2017

Barrier	%
Their ability to do the job	34%
The costs of making reasonable adjustments	31%
The inconvenience of making reasonable adjustments	19%
Fear of an increased possibility of litigation	13%
Their ability to integrate into the team	11%
A potentially negative customer reaction	9%
Not applicable – nothing in particular would be a barrier to my business hiring a person with a disability	34%
Employers who perceived a barrier	63%

Source: CSJ/YouGov

In addition, these two brackets do not capture all young people with disabilities.

Eligibility for financial support should be broadened so that it includes care leavers, people with EHC plans and disabled people as defined by the Equality Act 2010. Additional costs arising from this would be met through the apprenticeships levy.

Recommendation 2

We know that cost is another commonly perceived obstacle for employers when it comes to hiring disabled people. It is important to signal to employers that they can make cost-neutral decisions about disabled people and focus on their strengths, skills and attitudes.

Under current funding plans, employers and training providers who qualify for support will receive £1,000 to cover the additional costs associated with supporting apprentices who qualify for this help.

This figure should be revisited. The costs of supporting disabled people with different impairments vary substantially, as do funding bands for apprenticeships; the relative value of contributing £1,000 towards costs will therefore differ from case to case. It would be better to have a more flexible system of support that adjusts to specific needs and would instead cover the costs of making reasonable adjustments.

Disability correlates strongly with increasing age and the demographic balance of our population is tilting towards older age.

March 2017

⇨ The above extract is reprinted with kind permission from The Centre for Social Justice. Please visit www.centreforsocialjustice. org.uk for further information.

Paralysed people could walk again instantly after scientists prove brain implant works in primates

By Sarah Knapton, Science Editor

Paralysed people could walk again instantly after scientists developed a brain implant which turns thought into electrical signals in the spine so that lost feeling can be restored after injury.

Currently people who break their backs or suffer a spinal trauma are unable to stand or move even though their legs still work, because the signal which connects their brains to their muscles is disconnected.

But an international team of scientists have shown it is possible to bypass the injury and reconnect the brain signals to electrodes at an undamaged part of the spine.

Two monkeys who were temporarily paralysed in one leg were able to walk again instantly using the technique, which could be available for humans within a decade.

"For the first time, I can imagine a completely paralysed patient able to move their legs through this brain-spine interface, said neurosurgeon Jocelyne Bloch of the Lausanne University Hospital.

Neuroscientist Dr Erwan Bezard of Bordeaux University who oversaw the experiments added: "The primates were able to walk immediately once the brain-spine interface was activated. No physiotherapy or training was necessary."

Humans are able to move because electrical signals originating in the brain's motor cortex travel down to the lumbar region in the lower spinal cord, where they activate motor neurons that coordinate the movement of muscles responsible for extending and flexing the leg.

But injury to the upper spine can cut off communication between the brain and lower spinal cord.

To create a device which mimicked the natural communication of the brain and muscles, scientists needed to decode signals from the motor cortex and turn them into electronic signals which could fire electrodes and stimulate nerves in the spine.

The device works wirelessly so only two small implants are needed, one in the brain and one in the spine.

It was tested on two macaque monkeys with lesions that spanned half the spinal cord and who could not walk on one leg. When turned on, the animals began spontaneously moving their legs while walking on a treadmill.

"With the system turned on, the animals in our study had nearly normal locomotion," said Dr David Borton, assistant professor of engineering at Brown University and one of the study's co-lead authors.

Previous studies have shown that it is possible to use signals decoded from the brain to control movement of a robotic or prosthetic hands but it has never been shown to help stimulate muscles directly.

The researchers say not only could it help paralysed people to walk again, but in the long term may even encourage the regrowth of damaged circuits.

"There's an adage in neuroscience that circuits that fire together wire together," added Dr Borton.

"The idea here is that by engaging the brain and the spinal cord together, we may be able to enhance the growth of circuits during rehabilitation. That's one of the major goals of this work and a goal of this field in general."

The researchers say the device still has several limitations. Presently the signalling only works one way so sensations do not pass back to the brain and it is also unclear how much weight the legs can bear.

However British experts said the experiment was "very promising and exciting".

"It is an important step forward in our understanding of how we could improve motor recovery in patients affected by spinal cord injury by using brain-spinal interface approaches," said Professor Simone Di Giovanni, Chair in Restorative Neuroscience, Imperial College London.

"In principle this is reproducible in human patients. The issue will be how much this approach will contribute to functional recovery that impacts on the quality of life. This is still very uncertain."

Dr Andrew Jackson, of the Movement Laboratory at the Institute of Neuroscience, Newcastle University, added: "The idea of using electronic implants to bypass damaged neural pathways dates back to the 1970s but the twenty-first century has seen remarkable progress in this field.

"It is not unreasonable to speculate that we could see the first clinical demonstrations of interfaces between the brain and spinal cord by the end of the decade."

9 November 2016

⇨ The above information is reprinted with kind permission from *The Telegraph*. Please visit www.telegraph.co.uk for further information.

Paralysed man moves arms with thought-control tech

"It's better than I thought it would be."

By Sophie Gallagher, reporter at Huffington Post

A man in America is the first quadriplegic in the world to have his arm and hand movements restored after receiving a groundbreaking brain implant.

Bill Kochevar in Cleveland, Ohio was able to drink from a straw and feed himself mashed potato after his right arm was brought back to life by thought-control technology.

Kochevar said: "For somebody who's been injured eight years and couldn't move, being able to move just that little bit is awesome to me… it's better than I thought it would be."

The 56-year-old was completely paralysed below his shoulders after a cycling accident eight years ago, and has been unable to live without full-time care.

Now, as part of the BrainGate2 study at Case Western Reserve University, Kochevar has had surgery on his motor cortex, to implant two 'baby-aspirin-sized' pill electrodes on the surface of his brain.

These electrodes work by recording the brain activity neurons to generate signals and tell one of 36 electrodes on his upper and lower arms to stimulate the relevant muscles.

Before the surgery could be undertaken, Kochevar had to practise training his brain to remember the relevant signals on a computer.

But he was able to pick it up within minutes as the 'code' was still filed away in his memory, according to associate professor of neurology, Benjamin Walter.

Bob Kirsch, Chair of Case Western Reserve's University, said: "He's really breaking ground for the spinal cord injury community. This is a major step toward restoring some independence."

BrainGate2 is a pilot clinical trial that is exploring the feasibility of using brain-computer interfaces to help paralysed people with spinal injuries.

The first BrainGate study discovered that people with paralysis can control a cursor on a computer screen or a robotic arm.

29 March 2017

⇨ The above information is reprinted with kind permission from The Huffington Post UK. Please visit www.huffingtonpost.com for further information.

New gene therapy gives hope to people born with inherited eye disorder

An article from The Conversation.

By Sten Andreasson, Clinical Professor, Lund University

The first successful gene therapy for an inherited form of blindness was recently reviewed by an expert panel of advisers at US Food and Drug Administration (FDA). They unanimously voted in recommendation of the treatment. The FDA now has until 12 January, 2018 to approve the treatment.

Spark Therapeutics, an American biotech firm, developed the therapy (Luxturna) to treat Leber congenital amaurosis (LCA), an inherited eye disorder. Although LCA is very rare (affecting about one in 80,000 people) it is the most common cause of inherited sight loss in young people.

The disease causes cells in the eye, known as the retinal pigment epithelium, to stop working properly. This thin layer of cells supports and nourishes the retina, the light-sensitive tissue at the back of the eye.

LCA symptoms, such as night blindness, roving eyes (nystagmus) and tunnel vision, start in early childhood and usually progress to complete sight loss by the age of 18. There is currently no approved treatment for the disease.

Scientists have identified 20 different types of LCA, each caused by a different defective gene. The version of LCA that Luxturna treats is caused by a mutation of a gene called RPE65.

Luxturna is a one-off treatment involving injections of healthy RPE65 genes into the retina. The genes are carried by billions of modified, harmless viruses (so-called "viral vectors"). The healthy genes are then able to make the protein necessary for normal vision.

Clinical trials have demonstrated that patients experience benefits within one month of the procedure.

In a phase III clinical trial, researchers measured participants' ability to navigate obstacles under various light conditions, ranging from one lux (about the same as a moonless summer night) to 400 lux (similar to the light in an office). An analysis of the results showed that 93% of participants had clinically and statistically significant improvements in their vision – although the treatment does not completely restore sight. None of the trial participants reported serious side effects.

As would be expected, none of the people in the control group had any improvements in their vision. However, under the terms of the trial, the people in the control group are now eligible to receive the treatment.

If the treatment is approved by the regulator, it will be the first gene therapy for an inherited condition approved by the FDA. And it will probably open the door for other gene-therapy treatments for genetic eye disorders.

Analysts are already predicting the likely cost of the treatment. Given that it is a one-off treatment for a rare disease, the cost per patient could be as high as US$1 million.

Exciting new period

Gene therapy trials are currently underway for at least 15 different disease-causing genes responsible for different forms of retinal degeneration.

Scientists have reached this exciting stage of development in gene therapies for eye disorders thanks to the hard work of many researchers, but especially that of Jane Bennett and Albert Maguire, who, in 2008, published the results of the first gene therapy treatment in patients with LCA and mutation in the RPE65 gene.

Thanks to the work of these pioneers, and many others, we are now on the cusp of being able to offer hope to the thousands of patients who suffer from these debilitating inherited eye disorders.

16 October 2016

⇨ The above information is reprinted with kind permission from *The Conversation*. Please visit www.theconversation for further information.

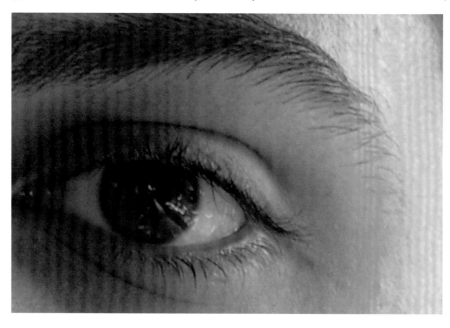

Oxford spinout develops smart glasses giving legally blind the ability to read and navigate

University spinout OxSight, has reported that in a recent UK-wide trial its smart glasses helped sight impaired and blind people to navigate independently, avoid collisions and see in the dark.

Participants reported that they were able to describe people standing several metres away and in some cases even recognise their faces and expressions.

OxSight also announced it has successfully raised a seed funding round from Oxford angel investor Mr Zhang Jiangong. The company will use the funding to continue to develop the smart glasses. Existing partners include Google, the Royal National Institute of Blind People, the University of Oxford, the NIHR i4i scheme, the Royal Academy of Engineering and Oxford University Innovation. Both Mr Zhang and RTC Innovation, a UK-based technology transfer company have provided valuable support to OxSight over the last three years.

The OxSight smart glasses use a unique camera system and computer vision algorithms to detect and highlight objects, separating them from the background in real time. This allows people with even the lowest amount of sight make better use of their vision in challenging everyday scenarios.

The technology was developed at Oxford's Nuffield Department of Clinical Neuroscience by visual prosthetics researcher Dr Stephen Hicks with support from the Oxford Eye Hospital. Hicks' team used their understanding of how the brain interprets visual information to develop algorithms that replicate our natural visual interpretation process.

OxSight founder Dr Stephen Hicks said: "About 90 per cent of legally blind people retain some residual vision. Our aim is to allow individuals to make the most of this. When a blind person puts on the OxSight Smart Specs they should be able to locate objects and people, recognise where they are and navigate more easily. They can avoid colliding with objects, walk confidently at a normal pace and have more meaningful interactions with friends and family. This can be incredibly empowering.

Behind these glasses is ten years of work developing a real-time computer vision algorithm that mimics some of the basic components of human visual perception. The algorithm detects the distance to nearby objects and forms a depth-map which is then enhanced and displayed on the inside of a pair of glasses. It highlights edges and features which make many objects easier to see, especially in low light where many people struggle.

Founder Professor Philip Torr from Oxford's Department of Engineering Science said: "Wearing the OxSight Smart Specs is as straightforward as putting on a pair of reading glasses. They don't require special training and they help immediately. Computer Vision and Machine Learning work at Oxford will continue to improve the product performance in coming months."

OxSight CEO Dr Rakesh Roshan said: "We aim to move swiftly to develop these glasses for the blind community to use day-to-day, greatly improving their independence. They have already given us valuable feedback and co-operation, and our aim is to hit our regulatory, technical and manufacturing milestones as quickly as possible."

Current versions of OxSight's smart glasses allow users to zoom in, change contrast and choose between a simple white highlight of objects and obstacles, through to enhanced edges and contrast, a cartoonised filter that can improve face detection and finally a bright and colourful image. All filters provide live video: as the user moves their head around, the images move too.

The images are displayed on transparent lenses, allowing the wearer to use their vision as normal while still seeing an enhanced overlay. Other people can still see the wearer's eyes, which helps in social situations.

Mr Zhang said: "OxSight offers immense value to society globally. It has been a great pleasure working with a very talented team at Oxford and we look forward to building new partnerships and making a significant impact."

In 2014, the Oxford/Royal National Institute of the Blind smart glasses project won a Google Impact Challenge.

Technology commercialisation company Oxford University Innovation assisted the researchers in protecting the intellectual property and commercialising the smart glasses. The technology is protected by patents, copyright and proprietary know how. RTC Innovation, a UK-based Chinese technology transfer company also provided valuable support.

Facts about blindness and visual impairment:

⇨ Around 39 million people worldwide are totally blind, 246

million have low vision and 285 million have some kind of visual impairment, according to the World Health Organization (2014)

⇨ The estimated cost of visual impairment to the UK annual health budget is more than £250 million

⇨ Common causes of loss of sight include Macular degeneration (AMD), diabetic retinopathy, glaucoma and retinitis pigmentosa.

⇨ The top five common issues for visually impaired individuals are driving, reading, seeing facial expressions, independent navigation and watching TV.

27 July 2016

⇨ The above information is reprinted with kind permission from the University of Oxford. Please visit www.innovation.ox.ac.uk for further information.

Disabled daughter's womb removed in growth-stunting therapy in New Zealand

The ten-year-old's parents are afraid that growing too big will radically reduce her quality of life.

By Jess Stauffenberg

A disabled girl who is unable to see, walk or speak has had her womb removed as part of growth-stunting therapy her parents hope will prolong her life.

Ten-year-old Charley Hooper, who was born without access to oxygen for the first hour of her life, will remain 1.3 metres tall and 24 kilogrammes in weight after receiving growth attenuation therapy, according to Global News.

Her family, who live in New Zealand, was afraid that as she grew older she might be in pain during puberty and need to be hoisted with machines.

Jen Hooper, Charley's mother, read a newspaper article in 2006 about a disabled girl in Seattle who had received the first case of growth attenuation.

The practice of receiving oestrogen to prevent breast growth and removing the womb to stop puberty had not been done before with a disabled person in New Zealand.

An Auckland ethics panel said the treatment was unnecessary, however, and would not allow it to go ahead.

Mrs Hooper was angry at this, saying many public places have no such "well developed" adaptations for disabled people.

"We didn't stomp on her human rights. As far as I'm concerned we did the opposite," said Mrs Hooper in interview with Global News.

"Surely she has a right to live as good a life as she can, as pain-free as she can, as involved and participatory as she can, and we feel like we've given her that."

Instead the family asked for the treatment to begin abroad and then have it continued in New Zealand, which the panel agreed to.

Hormones were first administered by a doctor in South Korea and completed by Paul Hofman, a paediatric endocrinologist at Starship Children's Hospital in Auckland.

He said that since the treatment, Charley is smiling more often, seems better able to move and that he has no regrets about the therapy.

But Margaret Nygren, CEO of the American Association on Intellectual and Developmental Disabilities, said that such therapy means "that you're keeping someone small for the convenience of those around them, not so the individual is able to have the most fulfilling life."

28 October 2015

⇨ The above information is reprinted with kind permission from *The Independent*. Please visit www.independent.co.uk for further information.

Virtual reality helped improve nerve function in paralysed people

"**V**irtual reality has helped eight paralysed patients regain some feeling in their legs in 'a big surprise'," Sky News reports.

Researchers using virtual reality (VR) combined with a robotic exoskeleton were surprised to find participants regained some nerve function.

The people, eight in total, with paralysis and loss of sensation of both legs (paraplegia), were taking part in the Walk Again Neurorehabilitation programme. Paraplegia is usually caused by a spinal injury so nerve signals from the brain cannot reach the legs.

The programme combined the use of an exoskeleton designed to respond to electrical signals of the brain with VR that provided both visual and haptic stimulation. Haptic refers to the sensation of touch; it is haptic technology that causes smartphone screens to 'respond' to your touch.

The technologies were combined to create a simulation of physical activity, such as taking part in a virtual football match.

Researchers expected the training would improve proficiency with using the exoskeleton. They were pleasantly surprised to discover it actually improved real-world nerve function.

All patients showed improvements in their ability to feel sensation and improved their control of key muscles as well as improving their ability to walk.

The researchers have hypothesised that the virtual activity could help rekindle nerve connections in the spine that have previously lain dormant.

Participants had been paralysed for between three to 15 years. The research team are now planning to use the same technique on people who have only been paralysed for a short time, to see if beneficial effects are more significant.

Where did the story come from?

The study was carried out by researchers from a number of institutions, including the Associação Alberto Santos Dumont para Apoio à Pesquisa, University of Munich, Colorado State University and Duke University. Funding for the study was provided by the Brazilian Ministry of Science, Technology and Innovation. The authors declared no conflicts of interest.

The study was published in the peer-reviewed journal *Science Reports*, on an open-access basis, so it is free to read online.

The UK media reported on these results accurately and included quotes from the study authors expressing their disbelief in what they saw. "In virtually every one of these patients, the brain had erased the notion of having legs. You're paralysed, you're not moving, the legs are not providing feedback signals," said Professor Nicolelis. He went on to say: "By using a brain-machine interface in a virtual environment, we were able to see this concept gradually re-emerging into the brain."

BBC News also hosts a short video of one of the participants, who had previously been paralysed for years, taking some tentative steps on a treadmill.

What kind of research was this?

This study is a case report of eight people with paraplegia that aimed to explore to what degree brain-machine interfaces, combined with a VR rig, could help people with spinal cord injuries regain their ability to walk by using a brain-controlled exoskeleton.

Paralysis is loss of the ability to move one or more muscles. It may be associated with loss of feeling and other bodily functions. In this study

participants had paraplegia – were paralysed in both legs. There aren't usually any problems with the leg muscles themselves, only somewhere along the course of transmitting sensory or motor nerve signals to or from the spinal cord and brain.

People with paraplegia are usually able to lead a relatively independent and active life, using a wheelchair to carry out their daily activities.

To establish whether this technology would work on a larger scale or on people with different levels of paralysis, further clinical trials would need to take place.

What did the research involve?

The researchers recruited eight people with paraplegia who had chronic spinal cord injury.

Participants wore caps fitted with electrodes to read their brain signals and were asked to imagine moving their arms to create brain activity. Once this was mastered, the participants learnt how to use their own brain signals to control an individual avatar or robotic leg by imagining that they were moving their own legs. They were 'connected' to the avatar through the use of a VR headset, that provided images, as well as a number of haptic sensors giving tactile feedback. So it both looked and felt like they were moving their legs.

These signals were read by the electrodes in the cap and used to control to the exoskeleton.

The researchers investigated more complex activities over the course of the study to ensure cardiovascular system stability and patient postural control. This involved various gait training robotic systems.

The six stages of activity were:

⇨ the patient was seated and their brain activity was recorded using an electroencephalogram (EEG) while they controlled the movements of a human body avatar in the VR environment

⇨ as above but whilst standing

⇨ training with body weight support system on a treadmill

⇨ training with body weight support system on an overground track

⇨ training with a brain-controlled robotic body weight support system on a treadmill

⇨ training using a brain-controlled robotic exoskeleton.

Clinical evaluations were carried out on the first day of the trial and then at 4, 7, 10 and 12 months. These evaluations included tests for:

⇨ level of impairment

⇨ temperature, vibration, pressure and sensitivity

⇨ muscle strength

⇨ trunk control

⇨ independence

⇨ pain

⇨ range of motion

⇨ quality of life

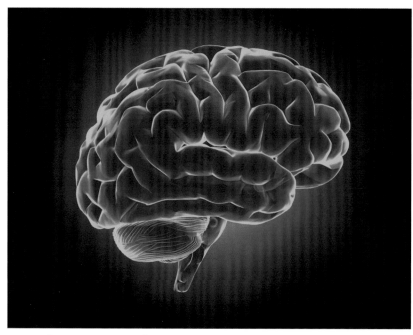

What were the basic results?

The eight participants in the study carried out 2,052 sessions, totalling 1,958 hours. After 12 months of training with robotic devices all patients made neurological improvements in terms of being able to feel pain and touch.

Patients also improved their control of key muscles and made improvements in their ability to walk. As a result of this study, half of the participants had their level of paraplegia changed from complete to incomplete.

How did the researchers interpret the results?

The researchers conclude: "Overall, the results obtained in our study suggest that [brain-machine interfaces, BMI] applications should be upgraded

from merely a new type of assistive technology to help patients regain mobility, through the use of brain-controlled prosthetic devices, to a potentially new neurorehabilitation therapy, capable of inducing partial recovery of key neurological functions.

"Such a clinical potential was not anticipated by original BMI studies. Therefore, the present findings raise the relevance of BMI-based paradigms, regarding their impact on SCI (spinal cord injury) patient rehabilitation. In this context, it would be very interesting to repeat the present study using a population of patients who suffered a SCI just a few months prior to the initiation of BMI training. We intend to pursue this line of inquiry next. Based on our findings, we anticipate that this population may exhibit even better levels of partial neurological recovery through the employment of our BMI protocol."

Conclusion

This study reported on the use of brain-controlled devices in eight people with paraplegia to establish whether they may be able to regain their ability to walk by using a brain-controlled exoskeleton.

The study found that all patients made neurological improvements in terms of being able to feel pain and touch and had improved their control of key

muscles and made improvements in their ability to walk.

These results would appear to chime with the known plasticity of the nervous system and brain. It can continue to change and adapt to different environmental stimulus. So it may be possible that damaged nerve pathways that have been dormant for many years could be rekindled through these types of activities.

However, whilst this technology is exciting and could provide hope for people with spinal cord injury, it is still in the very early stages. These findings are based on just eight people. Many more stages of testing will be needed in people with different causes and severities of paraplegia to confirm whether this does have true potential and who could gain most benefit. For now, it is too soon to know if and when it could become available.

The cost of VR technology continues to fall, while its sophistication continues to rise. So its use in mainstream rehabilitation at some point in the near future is certainly not in the realms of fantasy.

12 August 2016

⇨ The above information is reprinted with kind permission from NHS Choices. Please visit www.nhs.uk for further information.

Six amazing 3D-printed body parts that changed patients' lives

Ball's in your court, nature.

There's been a lot of hype around 3D printing, but its applications in medicine are real.

Advances in 'additive manufacturing' – the industrial version of 3D printing – are being applied toward federally approved medical devices, and have enabled surgeons from Scotland to Chicago to inexpensively visualise medical procedures before performing them. But that's far from all: doctors are also crafting personalised bones and joints for their patients.

The devices and materials used today in a medical context often go well beyond the plastic and resin prototypes commonly associated with 3D printing; though in both cases, machines add successive layers of materials together to form an object that can then be refined. The industrial-grade printers used for medical purposes or military manufacturing, however, use focused electron beams and powdered metal alloys to create parts, not plastic feedstock.

Medical researchers are now exploring how to print human tissue – so-called "bioprinting" – and building upon the basic science to enable doctors to make organs some day.

Here are six remarkable examples of body parts that 3D printers have already been used to create.

1. **A new craniumn**. In 2014, a Dutch woman received the first full 3D-printed skull implant. "Implants used to be made by hand in the operating theatre

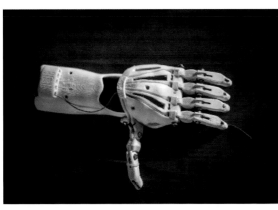

using a sort of cement which was far from ideal," Dr. Ben Verweij, a neurologist who led the medical team that crafted the prosthetic bone, told Dutch News. "Using 3D printing we can make one to the exact size. This not only has great cosmetic advantages, but patients' brain function often recovers better than using the old method."

2. **A new vertebra**. In 2014, a 12-year-old boy received the first-ever vertebra made on a 3D printer. The new bone was printed from titanium powder and featured a pocked surface, ensuring that his bones would fuse with the implant as he grew.

3. **Part of a rib cage**. This summer, a cancer patient in Spain received a titanium 3D-printed sternum and several ribs after his original bones were removed to excise a tumor. According to CNET, surgeons in Salamanca commissioned Anatomics, a medical device company in Australia, to create the customised implant.

4. **A nose for a girl born without one**. In the United Kingdom, a 3D printer will be used to build a nose for a little girl. The printed material will be implanted under her skin in stages, and a medical tattoo artist will give her nostrils and nose contours.

5. **A lifesaving airway for a baby**. In 2013, doctors at the University of Michigan used a 3D printer to create a splint for a baby boy born with a rare, potentially fatal condition that causes the airways near the lungs to collapse. "We custom designed Kaiba's splint using high-resolution images from a CT scan of Kaiba's trachea and the bronchus that was collapsing," wrote Glenn Green, one of the doctors

responsible for the device. "Using computer-aided design and a special laser-based 3-D printer, we produced the splint specifically to fit Kaiba's needs." In 2015, doctors have figured out how to make a 4D airway splint for babies. The fourth dimension refers to time, in this case. The breathing device grows with the child and then dissolves.

6. **A new arm**. While we're still a long way away from realising the full sci-fi future of Steve Austin and "The 6 Million Dollar Man" from the 1970s, partially 'bionic' men and women are now reality. Researchers and doctors have been developing increasingly robust bionic limbs – body parts that are stronger or more capable through electronic devices – for patients. (The field of bionics refers to "the study of mechanical systems that function like living organisms".) Since July, over a million people have watched a YouTube video of a girl named Isabella unpacking her new 3D-printed arm. It's still as heartwarming as ever.

Every year, these limbs are getting more and more affordable. In the future, some of these prosthetic limbs will be directly wired to the human brain, giving amputees and paralyzed people increased mobility and ability. That's the kind of mind control worth creating.

9 October 2015

⇨ The above information is reprinted with kind permission from The Huffington Post UK. Please visit www.huffingtonpost.co.uk for further information.

Key facts

- One billion of the world's population, or 15 per cent, live with a disability (page 1)

- Disabled people are at a higher risk of poverty in every country, whether measured in traditional economic indicators relative to GDP or, more broadly, in non-monetary aspects of living standards such as education, health and living conditions (page 1)

- Approximately 785 million women and men with disabilities are of working age, but the majority do not work (page 1)

- There are around 11.9 million disabled people in the UK. Almost one in five people (19%) in the UK have a disability; this figure has remained relatively constant over time (page 2)

- 44.3% of working age disabled people are economically inactive. This figure is nearly four times higher than for nondisabled people (11.5%) (page 2)

- The distribution of disabled people is fairly evenly spread across the UK. The North East, Wales, the North West and East Midlands have the highest rates of disability, while London, the South East and the East of England have the lowest (page 2)

- Disabled adults are nearly three times as likely as non-disabled adults to have no formal qualifications, 30% and 11%, respectively (page 2)

- 19% of households that include a disabled person live in relative income poverty (below 60% of median income), compared to 14% of households without a disabled person (page 2)

- 40% of disabled children in the UK live in poverty. This accounts for around 320,000 disabled children, and almost a third of those are classified as living in "severe poverty" (page 3)

- Arthritis affects one-fifth of adults in the UK, that's ten million people living with arthritis. (page 10)

- 79% (four in five) feel anxious or depressed because of their arthritis (page 10)

- There are an estimated 700,000 children and young people across the UK, some as young as five-years-old, who are caring for family members. This is likely a conservative figure as many are hidden from view (page 22)

- Most care for a parent or other close family member, day in, day out, and shockingly, at least 13,000 young carers are providing care for over 50 hours a week on top of their studies (page 22)

- According to a 2014 NHS survey of 11,000 pupils across the city, one in eight secondary school-age pupils in Glasgow is providing care for someone at home. Not only do these pupils care for someone with a disability, long-term illness, mental health or substance issue, they also have poorer outcomes for their own health and future expectations (page 23)

- Out-of-work benefits for disabled people cost £19 billion a year, while the Exchequer loses £21 billion–£29 billion a year in foregone tax and national insurance revenue due to health-related joblessness (page 26)

- Only a third (33 per cent) of employers have hired a disabled person in the last year, and fewer than one in ten (nine per cent) of employers think there is usually a strong business case for hiring a disabled person (page 26)

- The UK's disability employment gap is higher than that found in 21 other European countries, and those in Luxembourg, Sweden, France and Turkey are less than ten per cent (page 31)

- Around 39 million people worldwide are totally blind, 246 million have low vision and 285 million have some kind of visual impairment, according to the World Health Organization (2014) (page 36)

- The estimated cost of visual impairment to the UK annual health budget is more than £250 million (page 36)

- The top five common issues for visually impaired individuals are driving, reading, seeing facial expressions, independent navigation and watching TV (page 36)

- Advances in 'additive manufacturing' – the industrial version of 3D printing – are being applied toward federally approved medical devices, and have enabled surgeons from Scotland to Chicago to inexpensively visualise medical procedures before performing them. But that's far from all: doctors are also crafting personalised bones and joints for their patients (page 39)

Disability

The Equality Act 2010 defines a disabled person as anyone who has a physical or mental impairment that has a substantial and long-term adverse affect on his or her ability to carry out day-to-day activities (NHS Choices, 2012). The nature of the disability will determine the extent to which it impacts on an individual's daily life. The definition of disability includes both physical impairments, such as multiple sclerosis or blindness, and learning disabilities such as autism.

Hidden disabilities

Not all disabilities are obvious. An individual who suffers from epilepsy, mental ill health or diabetes still faces the challenge of coping with a disability but is often not recognised as a disabled person, since to a casual observer they do not display the outward symptoms often associated with disability.

Disability discrimination

The act of showing someone less favourable treatment (discriminating against them) because they have a disability. This may be through outright abusive behaviour, or by denying them access to employment, education or goods and services. The Equality Act 2010 states that it is illegal to discriminate against anybody because of a disability.

Independent Living Fund

The Independent Living Fund (ILF) provided money to help disabled people live an independent life in the community, rather than having to rely on residential care. Payments from the ILF could be used to: employ a carer or personal assistant to give you personal and domestic care, or to pay a care agency to provide personal care and help with domestic duties. A group of five disabled people are currently arguing against the Government's decision to abolish the ILF, claiming that 20,000 severely disabled people have been left in extreme difficulty and that their views were not taken into account when the decision was made to halt payments from March 2015 and stop accepting new claims.

Learning disabilities

Learning disabilities, sometimes called learning disorders or difficulties (although these terms can have a wider definition and it would be incorrect to use them interchangeably with 'learning disability'), are defined by the World Health Organization as 'a state of arrested or incomplete development of mind'. Learning disabilities affect a person's ability to learn, communicate and carry out everyday tasks. Autism and Asperger syndrome are two examples of learning disabilities. People with Down's syndrome will also have a learning disability. Learning disabilities were referred to as 'mental handicaps' in the past, but this definition is now considered obsolete and offensive.

Paralympic Games

The Paralympic Games are a series of sporting competitions open to athletes with physical disabilities. They are held immediately following the Olympic Games. Athletes with disabilities including amputations, paralysis and blindness take part in a wide range of competitive sports.

Assignments

Brainstorming

⇨ Brainstorm what you know about disability.

   • What types of disability are there?

   • What does the term 'paralysis' mean?

   • What is a young carer?

   • What do you understand by the term 'autism'?

Research

⇨ Do some research into the different types of disability that exist. You should consider both physical and mental disablities. Share your findings with the class.

⇨ In pairs, research accessibility for disabled people when attending sporting events. You should consider what problems they may face, and whether clubs are doing anything to help. Write a report on your findings which should be at least one page long.

⇨ Talk to friends and relatives to find out their thoughts on disabled people in the workplace. Do any of them work with a disabled person? Would they have any objections to working with a disabled person? Write a summary of your findings no longer than two pages long. Share with the rest of your class.

⇨ In small groups, do some research into 3D body parts. What types of parts can be printed and what different materials are used. Share your findings with the rest of your class.

⇨ Do some research into Autism. You should consider what age groups this condition affects. Does it affect one gender more than the other? Write a short report on your findings.

⇨ In pairs, research arthritis. How does this impact on people's everyday lives? Write a report of at least two A4 sides.

Design

⇨ In pairs, design a wheelchair friendly sports stadium. It should be a friendly, safe place to visit.

⇨ Design a poster to highlight the plight of child carers.

⇨ In pairs, design a sign to be displayed in a sports stadium directing disabled people to the areas which they can easily access.

⇨ Choose one of the articles from this book and create an illustration that highlights the key themes of the piece.

⇨ In small groups, design a wheelchair which is to be used by young children.

⇨ In pairs, design the interior of a bus which has space for both wheelchairs and pushchairs. Each area should be clearly marked and separate from each other.

⇨ You work for a company which has developed smart glasses for use by sight-impaired people and have been asked to design a new pair of glasses. Show your design to the rest of the class.

Oral

⇨ Have a class discussion about the lack of disabled toilets on trains. Consider how you might feel if you were disabled and there were no working facilities available to you. What do you think should be done to overcome this?

⇨ Split the class into two groups. Both groups should prepare a PowerPoint presentation that shows the different types of disability there are. Compare your findings with the other group.

⇨ In pairs, stage a discussion between two work colleagues. A new member of staff has been taken on who is disabled. You should discuss how this makes you feel.

⇨ As a class, look at the article on page 23 and discuss the issues facing young carers in the UK. Give your views on what could be done to help these children.

⇨ In small groups, discuss 'augmented reality to help disabled shoppers'. What does this term mean? Can you think of any other ways in which disabled shoppers could be helped?

Reading/writing

⇨ Write a one-paragraph definition of disability and share it with the rest of your class.

⇨ Read the article on page 15 and write a letter to your local bus company asking them how they intend to deal with this issue in the future.

⇨ 3D printers have changed patients' lives. Write an article exploring recent advances in this field.

⇨ "Employers may discriminate against autism without realising". Write an essay explaining this statement. You should write at least two sides of A4.

⇨ Read the article on page 32 and write down your thoughts regarding the use of such technology in helping paralysed people. Do you think it is right to use monkeys in this type of research? Write an essay at least two pages long giving your views on this.

Acknowledgements

The publisher is grateful for permission to reproduce the material in this book. While every care has been taken to trace and acknowledge copyright, the publisher tenders its apology for any accidental infringement or where copyright has proved untraceable. The publisher would be pleased to come to a suitable arrangement in any such case with the rightful owner.

Images

All images courtesy of iStock except pages 1 and 34: Morguefile, pages 15, 21, 36 and 39: Pixabay, page 19: Freepick.

Illustrations

Don Hatcher: pages 6 & 33. Simon Kneebone: pages 12 & 27. Angelo Madrid: pages 10 & 16.

Additional acknowledgements

With thanks to the Independence team: Shelley Baldry, Sandra Dennis, Jackie Staines and Jan Sunderland.

Tina Brand

Cambridge, January 2018